5-Minute Italian

Berlitz Publishing

New York   Singapore

5–MINUTE ITALIAN

Contacting the Editors
Every effort has been made to provide accurate information in this publication, but changes are inevitable. The publisher cannot be responsible for any resulting loss, inconvenience or injury. We would appreciate it if readers would call our attention to any errors or outdated information by contacting Berlitz Publishing, 193 Morris Avenue, Springfield, NJ 07081, USA. E-mail: comments@berlitzbooks.com

First Printing: October 2010
Printed in China
ISBN 978-981-268-625-1

Publishing Director: Sheryl Olinsky Borg
Senior Editor/Project Manager: Lorraine Sova
Cover Design: Leighanne Tillman, Claudia Petrilli
Writer: Dr. Emanuele Occhipinti
Reviewer: Chiara Marchelli
Composition: Wee Design Group
Production Manager: Elizabeth Gaynor
Cover Illustration: Leighanne Tillman

Contents

UNIT 1 Greetings and Introductions

UNIT 2 Nouns and Numbers

UNIT 3 Time and Date

UNIT 4 Family

UNIT 5 Meals

UNIT 6 Weather and Temperature

Contents

How to Use This Book

By using *5-Minute Italian* every day, you can start speaking Italian in just minutes. The 5-Minute program introduces you to a new language and gets you speaking right away. Take a few minutes before or after work, before you go to sleep at night or any time that feels right to work on one lesson a day. If you want, you can even go ahead and do two lessons a day. Just have fun while you learn; you'll be speaking Italian in no time.

- The book is divided into 99 lessons. Each provides a bite-sized learning opportunity that you can complete in minutes.

- Each unit has 8 lessons presenting important vocabulary, phrases and other information needed in everyday Italian.

- A review at the end of each unit provides an opportunity to test your knowledge before you move on.

- Unless otherwise noted, *5-Minute Italian* uses formal language. In everyday Italian, the formal is usually used between adults who are not close friends or family and in professional settings. The informal is used with friends and family and when addressing children.

Buon giorno!

- Real life language and activities introduce the vocabulary, phrases and grammar covered in the lessons that follow. You'll see dialogues, postcards, e-mails and other everyday correspondence in Italian.

- You can listen to the dialogues, articles, e-mails and other presentations on the *5-Minute Italian* audio CD.

5-Minute Italian audio

When you see this symbol , you'll know to listen to the specified track on the *5-Minute Italian* audio CD.

Smart Phrases

- In these lessons you'll find useful everyday phrases. You can listen to these phrases on the audio program.

- Extra Phrases enrich your knowledge and understanding of everyday Italian. These are not practiced in the activities, but they're there for those who want to learn more.

SMART TIP

Boxes like these are here to extend your Italian knowledge. You'll find extra language conventions and other helpful information on how to speak Italian.

Words to Know

- Core Words are important words related to the lesson topic. In some lessons these words are divided into sub-categories. You can listen to these words on our audio program.

- Extra Words are other helpful words to know.

Smart Grammar

- Don't let the name scare you. Smart Grammar covers the basic parts of speech you'll need to know if you want to speak Italian easily and fluently.

- From verb usage to forming questions, the 5-Minute program provides quick and easy explanations and examples for how to use these structures.

CULTURE TIP

Boxes like these introduce useful cultural information about Italian-speaking countries.

Unit Review Here you'll have a chance to practice what you've learned.

Challenge

Extend your knowledge even further with a challenge activity.

Internet Activity

- Internet activities take you to **www.berlitzbooks.com/5minute**, where you can test drive your new language skills. Just look for the computer symbol.

SMART PRONUNCIATION

Boxes like these demonstrate specific pronunciation tools. For example, did you know that the pronunciation of the letters *c* and *g* vary based on which vowel follows them? You'll learn more as you move further along in the book.

This section is designed to make you familiar with the sounds of Italian using our simplified phonetic transcription. You'll find the pronunciation of the Italian letters and sounds explained below, together with their "imitated" equivalents. Simply read the pronunciation as if it were English, noting any special rules below.

The accents ´ and ` indicate stress, e.g. *città*, cheet-<u>tah</u>. Some Italian words have more than one meaning. In these instances, the accent mark is also used to distinguish between them, e.g.: *é* (is) and *e* (and); *dà* (gives) and *da* (from).

Remember that all letters, with the exception of *h*, are sounded: this includes final vowels in words like *ragazzo*, *professore*, etc. Note also that double consonants are distinctly pronounced by holding (or lengthening) the sound.

Consonants

Letter	Approximate Pronunciation	Example	Pronunciation
c	1. before e and i soft sound like the English ch in chip	**centro**	chehn·troh
	2. before a, o, u hard sound like c in cat	**conto**	kohn·toh
ch	always hard sound like in cat	**che**	keh
g	1. before e and i, like j in jet	**valigia**	vah·<u>lee</u>·jyah
	2. before a, o, u, like g in get	**gatto**	<u>gaht</u>·toh
gg	pronounced more intensely	**viaggio**	vyah·dj·oh
gh	always hard sound like g in go	**ghiaccio**	<u>ghyah</u>·chyoh
gli	like lli as in million	**figlio**	<u>fee</u>·llyoh
gn	like the first n in onion	**bagno**	<u>bah</u>·nyoh
h	always silent	**ho**	oh
r	rolled at the back of the mouth	**Roma**	<u>roh</u>·mah
s	1. like s in same	**sole**	<u>soh</u>·leh
	2. sometimes, between two vowels, z as in zoo	**rosa**	<u>roh</u>·zah
sc	1. before e and i, sh as in shut	**uscita**	oo·<u>shee</u>·tah
	2. before a, o, u, sk as in skin	**scarpa**	<u>skahr</u>·pah
z/zz	1. generally ts as in hits	**grazie**	<u>grah</u>·tsyeh
	2. sometimes a little softer like dz as in zebra	**zero**	<u>dzeh</u>·roh

Letters b, d, f, l, m, n, p, q, t, v are pronounced as in English. The letters j, k, w, x and y are used in foreign origin words.

Vowels

Letter	Approximate Pronunciation	Example	Pronunciation
a	like the a in father	**gatto**	<u>gaht</u>·toh
e	1. like e in get 2. before a single consonant, sometimes like e in they	**destra** **sete**	<u>deh</u>·strah <u>say</u>·teh
i	like ee in meet	**sì**	see
o	1. like o in soft 2. like o in cold	**notte** **sole**	<u>noht</u>·teh <u>soy</u>·leh
u	like oo in food	**uno**	<u>oo</u>·noh

Vowel Combinations

ae	**paese**	pah·<u>eh</u>·zeh
ao	**Paolo**	<u>pah</u>·oh·loh
au	**auto**	<u>ow</u>·toh
eo	**museo**	<u>moo</u>·zeh·oh
eu	**euro**	<u>eh</u>·oo·roh
ei	**lei**	lay
ia	**piazza**	<u>pyah</u>·tsah
ie	**piede**	<u>pyeh</u>·deh
io	**io**	yoh
iu	**più**	<u>pyoo</u>
ua	**quale**	<u>kwah</u>·leh
ue	**questo**	<u>kweh</u>·stoh
ui	**qui**	kwee
uo	**può**	<u>pwoh</u>

In this unit you will:

- learn common phrases to greet and say goodbye.
- say your name and where you are from.
- learn personal pronouns and two uses of the verb *essere* (to be).
- learn common phrases and words about nationality.

LESSON 1

Buon giorno!

Dialogue

Lisa meets her new neighbor Marco. Listen as she introduces herself and asks Marco where he is from.

Lisa Buon giorno. Mi chiamo Lisa. Come si chiama?

Marco Mi chiamo Marco. Piacere!

Lisa Sono italiana. E Lei? Di dov'è?

Marco Sono svizzero.

Lisa Piacere di conoscerla.

Marco Anch'io. A presto!

SMART TIP

In conversations, speakers will drop the personal pronoun. For example, instead of *Io sono italiana*, you may say *Sono italiana*.

Activity A

Circle **T** for true and **F** for false.

1 This meeting happens during the day.   **T / F**

2 Marco is happy to meet Lisa.   **T / F**

3 Lisa is from Switzerland.   **T / F**

4 Marco is from Italy.   **T / F**

Activity B

Fill in the missing questions or statements with phrases from the dialogue.

Mi chiamo Lisa. _____?

Mi chiamo Marco. _____.

Sono italiana. E Lei? _____?

Sono _____.

CULTURE TIP

In Italy, friends and family members usually say hello with two kisses, one on each cheek.

SMART TIP

Sono italiana.
Sono italiano.

SMART TIP

In Italian, adjectives have masculine and feminine forms. When saying *Sono italiano/italiana*, for example, the gender must agree with the subject, in this case the speaker. A male would say *italiano*, and a female would say *italiana*.

Core Phrases

Ciao!	Hello!
Ciao! or Arrivederci!	Goodbye!
Buon giorno.	Good morning.
Buona sera.	Good evening.
Buona notte.	Good night.
Come si chiama?	What is your name?
Di dov'è?	Where are you from?

Extra Phrases

Come sta?	How are you?
Piacere	Nice to meet you.
or Piacere di conoscerla.	
Anch'io.	Likewise.

SMART TIP

In Italy, adults usually use the formal "you," *Lei*, when they meet someone for the first time or when they meet older people. Once they get to know each other, they can use the informal *tu*. Young people use the informal *tu* with each other; the informal is also used with children and family members.

Activity A

What do you say if you want to…

1 …say hello?

_____

2 …ask someone his/her name?

_____

3 …ask someone where he/she is from?

_____

4 …say goodbye?

_____

Activity B

For each picture write the appropriate Italian greeting: *Buon giorno, Buona sera* or *Buona notte*.

1 _____

2 _____

3 _____

LESSON 3
Words to Know

Core Words

Canada		Canada
Irlanda		Ireland
Italia		Italy
Regno Unito		United Kingdom
Stati Uniti		United States
Svizzera		Switzerland

America del Nord
North America

Europa
Europe

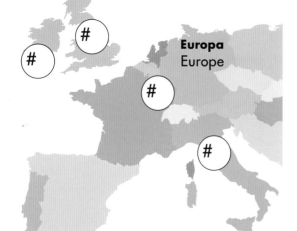

Activity A

Write the corresponding number on the maps for each country.

1 Svizzera
2 Regno Unito
3 Irlanda
4 Stati Uniti
5 Italia
6 Canada

Activity B

Match each flag to the name of the country.

1 Italia
2 Irlanda
3 Svizzera
4 Regno Unito

LESSON 4
Smart Grammar

Personal Pronouns

io	I
tu	you (inf.)
Lei	you (form.)
lui/lei	he/she
noi	we
voi	you (pl.)
loro	they

Abbreviations

masculine	m	singular	sing.	informal	inf.
feminine	f	plural	pl.	formal	form.

Activity A

Write the correct singular pronoun under each picture.

1 _____
I

2 _____
she

3 _____
he

4 _____
you (inf.)

Activity B

Write the correct plural pronoun under each picture.

1 ____*voi*____
you (pl.)

2 ____*loro*____
they

3 _____
we

Activity C

Write the pronoun you use when talking about…

1 …yourself. ____*io*____
2 …a woman. ____*Lei*____
3 …a man. ____*lui*____
4 …yourself plus your family. ____*noi*____
5 …a group of people. ____*voi*____

SMART TIP

Remember that in writing the formal "you", *Lei*, is capitalized so that it is not confused with "she", *lei*.

Di dov'è?

Lingua e nazionalità

L'italiano è la lingua ufficiale di quattro paesi in Europa: Italia, Città del Vaticano, San Marino e la parte meridionale della Svizzera. È anche la seconda lingua ufficiale in alcune parti della Croazia e della Slovenia. Ogni paese in cui si parla l'italiano ha la propria nazionalità. Così come qualcuno del Canada è canadese, non inglese, qualcuno della Svizzera è svizzero, non italiano. Questa tabella mostra alcuni esempi di paesi, di nazionalità e delle loro lingue.

Paese	Nazionalità	Lingua
Croazia	croata	croato italiano
Svizzera	svizzera	italiano francese tedesco
Italia	italiana	italiano
Slovenia	slovena	sloveno italiano

Language and Nationality

Italian is the official language of four countries in Europe: Italy, Vatican City, San Marino and the southern part of Switzerland. It is also the second official language in some parts of Croatia and Slovenia. Each country where Italian is spoken has its own nationality. Just as someone from Canada is Canadian, not English, someone from Switzerland is Swiss not Italian. The table above shows some examples of countries, nationalities and their languages.

Where are you from?

Read the article about Italian-speaking countries and nationalities—don't worry if you can't understand every word, but try to get the gist of the story. Underline the Italian words that are familiar or similar to any words in English. Then read the English translation.

Activity A

Complete the bilingual chart with words from the article. The first one is done for you.

country	paese
language	
nationality	
Italian	
English	

Activity B

Cover the English translation of the article. Read the Italian article again and circle the correct answer.

1 Italian is the official language in 4

    a paesi   **b lingue**

2 People in the southern part of Switzerland speak

    a svizzero   **b italiano**

3 Someone from Canada is

    a inglese   **b canadese**

4 Someone from Croatia is

    a italiano   **b croato**

> **SMART TIP**
>
> Words for nationality and language are not capitalized in Italian unless they are at the beginning of a sentence. For example, in English we write "I am Italian. I speak Italian." In Italian, we write *Sono italiano. Parlo italiano.*

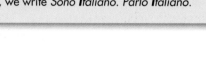

LESSON 6

Words to Know

Core Words

americano/americana	American (m/f)
australiano/australiana	Australian (m/f)
canadese	Canadian
inglese	English
italiano/italiana	Italian (m/f)
svizzero/svizzera	Swiss (m/f)

Extra Words

irlandese	Irish
francese	French
portoghese	Portuguese
tedesco/tedesca	German (m/f)

Activity A

Choose the correct nationality for each person.

1 (Swiss) Teresa è _____.
   svizzera/italiana

2 (American) Sarah è _____.
   inglese/americana

3 (English) Tim è _____.
   inglese/canadese

4 (Australian) Matthew è _____.
   australiano/inglese

Activity B

Use the vocabulary from the word box to identify each dish's nationality.

> canadese   inglese   americana
>   italiana   svizzera

1 _____

2 _____

3 _____

4 _____

5 _____

SMART TIP

Most adjectives that end in -o and -a in Italian have a masculine and feminine form. Adjectives that end in -e can either be masculine or feminine. For example, "American" is either *americano* (m) or *americana* (f). A man says *Sono americano*. A woman says *Sono americana*. In Activity B, the feminine forms *americana, italiana e svizzera* are used because you were identifying the food's *nazionalità* (nationality).

LESSON 7
Smart Phrases

SMART TIP

The Italian adjective for "English" is also the word for the language. For example, an English person would say *Sono inglese* (I am English) and *Parlo inglese* (I speak English). Keep in mind, though, that if the adjective for the nationality is gender specific, the male form of the adjective is the word for the language. For example, an Italian woman would say *Sono italiana e parlo italiano* (I am Italian and I speak Italian).

Core Phrases

È inglese?	Are you English?
Sono canadese.	I'm Canadian.
Parla italiano?	Do you speak Italian?
Un po'.	A little.
Parlo bene/male.	I speak well/poorly.

Activity A

What do you say if you want to…

1   …ask someone if he's Italian?

_____

2   …say you speak a language well?

_____

3   …say you speak a little?

_____

Your Turn

Imagine you just met someone while traveling in Italy. Use the phrases and vocabulary you've learned to create a dialogue. Ask about the person's nationality and the language he/she speaks. Write your questions in the You column. Write the answers in the Person From Italy column.

You	Person From Italy
Q1	A1
Q2	A2

CULTURE TIP

In Italy people tend to use the diminutive when they are referring to small quantities. For example, if someone speaks a little English, he/she might say *un pochino* instead of *un po'*.

LESSON 8

Smart Grammar

The verb *essere* (to be)

The verb *essere* has several uses, including:

- introducing yourself or another person

- telling where a person is from and the person's nationality

Singular

io	sono	I am
tu	sei	you are (inf.)
Lei	è	you are (form.)
lui/lei	è	he/she is

Examples

Io sono Lisa.	I am Lisa.
Lui è Marco.	He is Marco.

Activity A

Fill in the blanks with the correct form of the verb *essere*.

1 Io _____ italiano.

2 Lei _____ svizzero.

3 Tu _____ americano.

4 Lei _____ canadese.

SMART TIP

In Italian, the adjective agrees with the subject in gender (masculine or feminine) and number. Endings change between masculine and feminine and between singular and plural. For example:

Massimo è italiano.
Massimo e Maurizio sono italiani.
Laura è americana.
Mary e Laura sono americane.

Plural

noi	siamo	we are
voi	siete	you are
loro	sono	they are

Examples

Noi siamo svizzeri.	We are Swiss.

Activity B

Fill in the blanks with the correct form of the verb *essere*.

1 Voi _____ americani.

2 Noi _____ svizzeri.

3 Loro _____ inglesi.

Your Turn

Maria, Giuseppe and Paola are getting to know each other. Complete their conversation with the correct form of the verb *essere*.

Giuseppe (to Maria) Di dov' _____?

Maria (to Diego and Paola) _____ svizzera. E voi, _____ italiani?

Giuseppe _____ italiano e Paola _____ croata.

Activity A

Complete the following chart.

Nome	Paese	Nazionalità
Laura		italiana
Massimo	Svizzera	
Cassandra		canadese
Brian	Stati Uniti	
Katie		inglese

Activity B

Using the verb *essere*, write a complete sentence saying where each person is from.

Example Paulina, Regno Unito:
Paulina è inglese.

1 tu, Stati Uniti: _____

2 Lisa, Italia: _____

3 Lei, Canada: _____

4 Adriano, Italia: _____

Activity C

Kiko is visiting Italy. Complete the dialogue as he speaks with his *guida turistica* (tourist guide).

Guida _____! Benvenuto in Italia!

Kiko Buon giorno. _____ Kiko Buxó.
_____ Lei?

Guida _____ Enrico. Piacere.

Kiko Piacere. _____ italiano?

Guida Sì. _____?

Kiko _____ inglese.
_____?

Guida Un po'.

Kiko Parlo _____ e _____.

Guida Bene!

Kiko _____, Enrico.

Guida Arrivederci!

Activity D

Find the countries and the nationalities from the box in the word search. They may be written forward, backward, upside down or diagonally.

> Italia   Canada   Svizzera   italiano
> Regno Unito   Irlanda   canadese

```
L O S V I Z Z E R A U N I D A S
A Y P I T S U R N C I A S P D B
D C A N A D E S E D A Z H A N O
A L O O L P S E U D I T A P A C
N V N I I L T U R E P C Z O L I
A U C C A N A D A N S E Y L R X
R E G N O U N I T O N W R O I C
E L R E I N O N A I L A T I D M
```

Challenge

Can you find the Italian term for *Croatia* in the word search? Write it below.

Croatia _____

Activity E

Correct the error in each sentence. Write the correct version of the sentence on the line provided.

1 Arrivederci. Mi chiamo Laura.
_____

2 Noi sono canadesi. _____

3 Io sei italiano. _____

4 Manuel è americana.
_____

5 Parlo canadese. _____

6 Anna è italiano. _____

Internet Activity

Are you interested in learning more Italian names? Go to **www.berlitzbooks.com/5minute** for a list of sites with Italian names. Browse and pick three or four names, each starting with a different letter. Practice saying those names. Try saying *Mi chiamo…* in front of each one.

In this unit you will:

- use vocabulary for people, animals and things, and the numbers 1–30.
- learn the differences between masculine and feminine, and singular and plural nouns.
- use the definite articles and regular *–are* and *–ere* verbs.
- practice filling in a form with information about yourself.
- learn how to ask for a telephone number and an address.

LESSON 1

La cartolina

A Postcard from Italy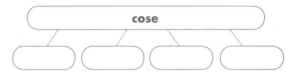

Look at the front and back of *la cartolina* (the postcard). Read the text, then circle the words that name people, things or animals.

Cara Rosa,

I'm having a great time in Italy, and I'm finally learning some Italian. Look at this postcard! Guarda la cartolina! Guarda gli animali. There are gatti e cani. Guarda le persone! There are bambini, bambine, uomini e donne. This is a very nice place. I like the case and edifici very much. Guarda le macchine e gli autobus. They are so colorful! This cartolina shows you le persone, gli animali e le cose I'm seeing.

I miss you. Mi manchi.
PS: How's my italiano?

      Robert

Ms. Rosa Martinelli
Box 219
Anaheim, California
U. S. A.

Activity A

Circle **T** for true and **F** for false.

1   Robert is visiting Switzerland.   **T / F**

2   Robert's postcard describes mountains and rivers.   **T / F**

3   Robert likes the houses and buildings.   **T / F**

4   The postcard describes colorful cars and buses.   **T / F**

Activity B

Write the Italian words that name…

1   …people in the postcard.

> **persone**

2   …things in the postcard.

> **cose**

3   …animals in the postcard.

> **animali**

Extension Activity

If you know more words for people, animals and things add them to the word webs above.

SMART TIP

Notice how all the words for people, animals and things in the postcard end with an *–i* or *–e*. This is because they are all in the plural form. The singular forms of the words are: *gatto, cane, bambino, bambina, uomo* (the pl. *uomini* is irregular), *donna, casa, edificio, macchina*. The word *autobus* doesn't change form because of foreign origin.

SMART TIP

Nouns in Italian are either feminine or masculine. Most nouns ending in *–a* are feminine, like *faccia* (face). Most nouns ending in *–o*, are masculine, like *toro* (bull). Nouns ending in *-e* can be either masculine, like *padre* (father), or feminine, like *madre* (mother), so you need to memorize their gender. Nouns ending in a consonant like *bar* (bar) are usually masculine, and stay the same in the singular and plural forms.

Core Words

la bambina	il bambino	l'uomo	la donna
girl	boy	man	woman

l'uccello	il gatto	il cane
bird	cat	dog

l'autobus	la macchina
bus	car

la strada	la casa	l'edificio
street	house	building

CULTURE TIP

There are two ways to say the word car: *la macchina* and *l'auto*. *Auto*—even though it ends in *-o*—is a feminine word; this is because it's the diminutive of the longer feminine word *automobile*.

Activity A

Write the Italian word for each item in the pictures.

1

2

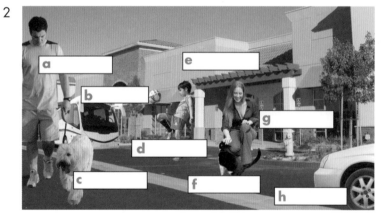

Activity B

Write *femminile* (feminine) or *maschile* (masculine) to classify each noun.

1 cane _____

2 bambino _____

3 macchina _____

4 strada _____

5 edificio _____

6 casa _____

7 gatto _____

8 autobus _____

LESSON 3

Smart Phrases

Core Phrases

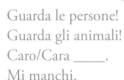

Guarda le persone!	Look at the people!
Guarda gli animali!	Look at the animals!
Caro/Cara _____.	Dear _____. (m/f)
Mi manchi.	I miss you.

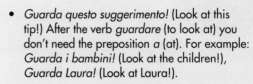

SMART TIPS

- *Guarda questo suggerimento!* (Look at this tip!) After the verb *guardare* (to look at) you don't need the preposition *a* (at). For example: *Guarda i bambini!* (Look at the children!), *Guarda Laura!* (Look at Laura!).

- If you want to be formal in your conversation, use *Guardi...!* instead of *Guarda...!*

Activity A

Laura is walking with Ernesto. As they walk, she points at people and things. Write a phrase in each speech balloon to indicate what Laura shows Ernesto.

1 _____
_____

2 _____
_____

Activity B

Fill in the blanks in Italian to help Laura write a postcard to her friend.

_____ Elena,

I'm having a great time here, and I'm learning

some _____. _____ le persone!

There are _____, _____ e _____.

Guarda le _____! Guarda l' _____! _____

gli animali! There are _____, _____ e _____.

Mi _____.

Laura

LESSON 4

Smart Grammar

Singular and Plural Nouns

To make the plural of a noun, change the final vowel. With nouns of foreign origin that end in a consonant, like *computer*, or words with an accented vowel, like *città* (city), the final vowel doesn't change.

- -a changes into -e: *casa/case* (house/houses).
- -o changes into -i: *ragazzo/ragazzi* (boy/boys).
- -e changes into -i: *notte/notti* (night/nights).

Activity A

Write the plural form of the nouns.

1 bambino _____

2 borsa  _____

3  matita _____

4 toro  _____

Definite Articles

The definite article (the) in Italian varies with the gender and number of the noun.

il	(m, sing. before nouns that begin with a consonant)
l'	(m, and f, sing. in front of a noun that begins with a vowel)
lo	(m, sing. with a noun that begins with s + consonant, z, ps)
la	f, sing.
i	m, pl. before nouns that begin with a consonant
gli	m, pl. before nouns that begin with a vowel, s + consonant, z, ps
le	f, pl.

Activity B

Write the correct definite article next to each noun.

1 _____ bambino
2 _____ strada
3 _____ cani
4 _____ donne
5 _____ matita
6 _____ autobus

Activity C

Look at the pictures and write the corresponding nouns with the correct definite articles.

1 _____

2 _____

3 _____

4 _____

Your Turn

See if you can guess the article of each new noun.

1 _____ penne (pens)
2 _____ zii (uncles)
3 _____ esame (exam)
4 _____ zoo (zoo)
5 _____ libro (book)

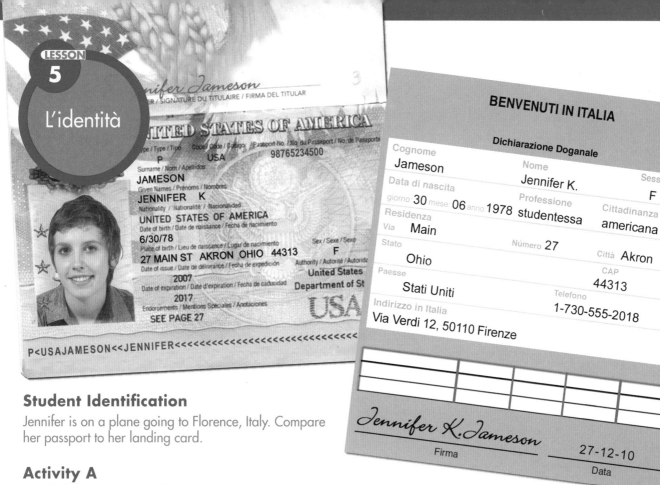

L'identità

LESSON 5

Student Identification

Jennifer is on a plane going to Florence, Italy. Compare her passport to her landing card.

Activity A

Match the Italian word with its English equivalent.

1	indirizzo	**a**	date of birth
2	via	**b**	last name
3	cognome	**c**	address
4	data di nascita	**d**	street

Activity B

Jennifer will be studying Italian at a school in Florence. Use the information above to complete the address section of her application.

CULTURE TIP

Outside the U.S., the date is usually written as day/month/year. So June 30, 2010 would be 30/06/10. When writing an address, the house or building number often comes after the street name. For example, 987 Washington Avenue is *Viale Washington 987*.

MODULO D'ISCRIZIONE

- -

Indirizzo in Italia:

Numero: _____

Via: _____

Stato: _____

Città: _____

LESSON 6

Words to Know

Core Words

I numeri (Numbers)

zero	0	undici	11
uno	1	dodici	12
due	2	tredici	13
tre	3	quattordici	14
quattro	4	quindici	15
cinque	5	sedici	16
sei	6	diciassette	17
sette	7	diciotto	18
otto	8	diciannove	19
nove	9	venti	20
dieci	10	trenta	30

Dati personali (Personal Information)

il viale	avenue
la via	street
l'indirizzo	address
il telefono	telephone

Activity A

Identify the pattern in the words *diciassette, diciotto* and *ventuno, ventidue, ventitré*.
Then write the Italian words to complete the number sequences.

sedici, diciassette, diciotto, _____, venti

ventuno, ventidue, ventitré, _____, _____, _____, _____, _____, _____, trenta

Activity B

Read the numbers 1–30 aloud in Italian. Then match each number with the correct word below.

1	dieci	4	dodici
6	uno	9	quindici
13	trenta	12	quattordici
18	sei	15	quattro
10	tredici	22	ventidue
30	diciotto	14	nove

Activity C

Translate the following information from Italian to English.

1 Via Verdi quattordici

_____

2 Viale Leopardi, numero ventisette

_____

3 Tel. zero-due, ventidue-quattordici-dieci

_____

4 CAP nove-sette-zero-diciannove

_____

SMART TIP

Watch out for these common abbreviations in Italian:

numero	N.
codice di avviamento postale	CAP
telefono	Tel.

Consolato
N. 29
Via Verdi 156
50100 Firenze
Tel. 055 21 34 56

CULTURE TIP

Italian phone numbers can vary. Usually, the area code is phrased in single digits (for example, 02, 055) and the number in two digit sets (for example, 22-19-10).

LESSON 7

Smart Phrases

Core Phrases

Qual è il suo numero di telefono?	What's your phone number?
Qual è il suo indirizzo?	What's your address?
Qual è il suo indirizzo e-mail?	What's your e-mail?
Quand'è il suo compleanno?	When's your birthday?
Vivo in/a ___.	I live in ___.
Il mio indirizzo è___.	My address is ___.
Il mio indirizzo e-mail è ___.	My e-mail is ___.
Il mio compleanno è___.	My birthday is ___.
Il mio numero di telefono è___.	My phone number is ___.
Dove vive?	Where do you live?

Activity A

Write your *nome, data di nascita, indirizzo* and *numero di telefono* in Italian.

nome _____

data di nascita _____

indirizzo _____

_____

numero di telefono _____

Activity B

What is Stefania asking Paolo? Circle the correct answer.

1

Dove vive?

a the place where he lives
b the place where he works

2

Qual è il suo indirizzo?

a the place where he lives
b his phone number

3

Qual è il suo numero di telefono?

a his phone number
b his date of birth

4

Quand'è il suo compleanno?

a his phone number
b his date of birth

Regular Verbs in the Present Tense

Regular verbs in Italian end in -are, -ere or -ire in the infinitive. Look at the chart to see how to conjugate verbs in the present tense with -are and -ere. You will learn verbs with -ire in the next unit.

Verbs with -are

Drop the –are and add the appropriate ending for each pronoun, such as with *parlare* (to speak).

io	parl**o**	I speak
tu	parl**i**	you speak
Lei	parl**a**	you speak
lui/lei	parl**a**	he/she speaks
noi	parl**iamo**	we speak
voi	parl**ate**	you speak
loro	parl**ano**	they speak

Examples Io parlo. I speak.
Noi parliamo. We speak.

Activity A

Conjugate the verb *parlare* in the present tense.

io _____

tu _____

lui/lei _____

noi _____

voi _____

loro _____

SMART TIP

When you name a series of things you can use the conjunction *e* (and): *Parlo italiano, inglese e spagnolo* (I speak Italian, English and Spanish).

Verbs with -ere

Drop the -ere and add the appropriate ending for each pronoun, such as with *vivere* (to live).

io	viv**o**	I live
tu	viv**i**	you live
Lei	viv**e**	you live
lui/lei	viv**e**	he/she lives
noi	viv**iamo**	we live
voi	viv**ete**	you live
loro	viv**ono**	they live

Examples Tu vivi. You live. (sing.)
Voi vivete. You live. (pl.)

Activity B

Conjugate the verb *vivere* in the present tense.

io _____

tu _____

lui/lei _____

noi _____

voi _____

loro _____

Activity C

Look at the pictures. Write in Italian where each person lives. Be sure to use the appropriate conjugation of *vivere*.

  Tom, 10 Orchard Street

_____

  Julia and Max, 24 Providence Street

_____

  Laura and I, 16 Main Street

_____

Your Turn

Think about the verb *insegnare* (to teach). How would you say in Italian that you teach English and Italian? How would you say that Laura teaches English?

Unit 2 | Review

Activity A

How many of each do you see? Use the correct plural form when necessary.

1  _____

2 _____

3 _____

4 _____

Activity B

Tom Wolf 25 Huron Street	482 913 7391
Laura Johnson 15 Columbia Street	+44 828 227 1984
Andrea White 8 4th Avenue	+44 20 2278 3625
Corrine & Mark Smith 30 4th Street	716 548 3549

Use the address book to answer the following questions. Remember that in Italian the order of some words may change.

1 Dove vive Andrea?

2 Qual è il numero di telefono di Tom? (use the word form)

3 Dove vivono Corrine e Mark?

4 Qual è il numero di telefono di Laura?

5 Dove vive Tom?

Activity C

Look at each noun and write the correct article. Don't forget to think about the number and gender of each noun. Then say a phrase with *Guarda!* to show each item or items.

1 _____ uccelli   3 _____ autobus

2 _____ donne   4 _____ zio

> **Challenge**
>
> Use a dictionary to look up *camminare* and *leggere*. Write two sentences for each verb using the pronouns *lui* and *loro*.

Activity D

You've just arrived at the Dante Alighieri Language Institute's office to study Italian. Laura, the receptionist, needs some basic information. She doesn't understand English, so you must respond in Italian. Complete the conversation.

Laura Buon giorno. Come si chiama?

Lei _____

Laura Bene. Qual è il suo numero di telefono?

Lei _____

Laura Qual è il suo indirizzo?

Lei _____

Laura E il codice di avviamento postale?

Lei _____

Laura Infine, qual è la sua data di nascita?

Lei _____

Laura Benissimo! Benvenuto all'Istituto di Lingue Dante Alighieri.

Lei _____

Internet Activity

Go to **www.berlitzbooks.com/5minute** for a list of map-related websites with satellite features in Italian. When you find one, type Istituto Dante Alighieri, Firenze. Zoom in on the map and write down all the information (address, zip code, telephone number, etc.). Practice saying the information aloud.

Unit 3 Time and Date

In this unit you will:
- tell *l'ora* (the time) and *la data* (the date).
- learn the numbers 31 and up.
- conjugate regular *–ire* verbs.
- learn the irregular verb *fare* (to do).

LESSON 1

Che ore sono?

Dialogue

Diana and Massimo are watching a soccer game. Listen to them talk about the time, how much time is left, how long the game is and the score.

Diana Che ore sono?

Massimo Sono le diciotto e trentacinque.

Diana È presto! Quanto tempo manca alla fine della partita?

Massimo Mancano cinquantacinque minuti. La partita dura novanta minuti.

Diana Qual è il punteggio?

Massimo Roma 1, Lazio 0

Activity A

Write the correct answer in Italian.

1 What time is it?

   _____

2 How much time is left in the game?

   _____

3 How long is the game?

   _____

4 Which team is winning?

   _____

Activity B

Put the dialogue in order. Number the phrases 1–4.

È presto! Quanto tempo manca alla fine della partita? #

Sono le diciotto e trentacinque. #

Mancano cinquantacinque minuti. #

Che ore sono? #

CULTURE TIP

In Italy, like most parts of Europe, the time is read according to the 24-hour clock. For example, 6:35 PM (*sei e trentacinque*) is 18:35 (*diciotto e trentacinque*). However, the 24-hour clock is mostly used for official schedules: trains, buses, planes, televisions, radios and movies. When using the 12-hour clock, be sure to include *di sera* after the p.m. time.

LESSON 2

Smart Phrases

Core Phrases

Che ore sono? or Che ora è?	What time is it?
Sono le due di notte.	It's 2 AM.
È l'una di notte.	It's 1 AM.
È mezzogiorno.	It's noon.
È mezzanotte.	It's midnight.
Sono le dieci di sera.	It's 10 PM.
Sono le sette e mezzo.	It's 7:30.
Sono le sei e un quarto.	It's a quarter after 6.
Sono le sette meno un quarto.	It's a quarter to 7.
È tardi!	It's late!
È presto!	It's early!

Activity A

Look at the clock and write a sentence telling what time it is.

Example
Sono le diciannove e quindici.

1 _____

2 _____

3 _____

4 _____

Activity B

You are supposed to meet a friend at *otto in punto di sera* (8:00 PM sharp). Look at the time and tell whether it is early or late. Write *È presto!* or *È tardi!*

1 Sono le sette meno un quarto. _____

2 Sono le otto e un quarto. _____

3 Sono le sette e mezzo. _____

4 Sono le nove. _____

Activity C

What do you say if you want to...

1 ...ask for the time?

_____

2 ...say it's early?

_____

3 ...say it's late?

_____

4 ...say it's 2 AM?

_____

SMART TIPS

- When using the 24-hour clock, for 15, 30 and 45 minutes past the hour you need to use *e quindici, e trenta* and *e quarantacinque*. So, for example, 18:15: *Sono le diciotto e quindici*; 16:30: *Sono le sedici e trenta*; 19:45: *Sono le diciannove e quaratacinque*.

- With the 12-hour clock, use *un quarto, e mezzo* and *meno un quarto* or *e tre quarti*. For example, 6:15: *Sono le sei e un quarto*; 4:30: *Sono le quattro e mezzo*; 7:45: *Sono le otto meno un quarto* or *Sono le sette e tre quarti*.

LESSON 3
Words to Know

Core Words

Il tempo (Time)

l'ora	hour
il minuto	minute
il secondo	second
in punto	o'clock/sharp

I numeri (Numbers)

trentuno	thirty-one
trentadue	thirty-two
trentatré	thirty-three
trentaquattro	thirty-four
trentacinque	thirty-five
trentasei	thirty-six
trentasette	thirty-seven
trentotto	thirty-eight
trentanove	thirty-nine
quaranta	forty
cinquanta	fifty
sessanta	sixty

Extra Words

mezzo	half
un quarto	quarter

SMART TIP

Numbers between the tens (30, 40, 50, etc.) follow a pattern, for example, *trenta* (30) + *due* (2) = *trentadue* (32). Did you notice the exceptions? The final vowel of the tens is dropped before *-uno* and *-otto*, and an accent is added to *-tre*, so, for example, numbers 31, 33 and 38 are: *trentuno, trentatré, trentotto*. Can you guess what 41, 43 and 48 are in Italian?

Activity A

Write the following numbers in word form.

1   44   _____

2   32   _____

3   67   _____

4   58   _____

Activity B

Quanto tempo manca? A show starts at *le venti in punto*. How much time is left until the show? Write the time in word form. Use *manca* for singular and *mancano* for plural. Also be sure to use the plural of *ora* and *minuto* when the answer is more than one.

Example

Manca un'ora. **or**
Mancano sessanta minuti.

Quanto manca?

1   _____

2   _____

3   _____

4   _____

Your Turn

It's 4:12 PM and you are watching a soccer game. The first half started at 4 PM and it lasts 45 minutes. You look at the clock every ten minutes.

Tell the time and how many minutes are left in the first half each time you look at the clock. Start at 4:12 PM.

LESSON 4

Smart Grammar

Regular Verbs in the Present Tense

Verbs with *-ire*

To conjugate regular *-ire* verbs such as *dormire* (to sleep), drop the *-ire* and add an ending as follows:

io	dorm**o**	I sleep
tu	dorm**i**	you sleep
Lei	dorm**e**	you sleep
lui/lei	dorm**e**	he/she sleeps
noi	dorm**iamo**	we sleep
voi	dorm**ite**	you sleep
loro	dorm**ono**	they sleep

Examples	Lui dorme.	He sleeps.
	Loro dormono.	They sleep.

Activity A

Complete the following chart to conjugate the verb *partire* (to leave) in the present tense.

io _____

tu _____

Lei _____

lui/lei _____

noi _____

voi _____

loro _____

SMART TIP

There is another group of *-ire* verb such as *capire* (to understand), to which *-isc* is added to the *io, tu, Lei, lui/lei, loro* forms before the regular ending:

io	cap**isco**	I understand
tu	cap**isci**	you understand
Lei	cap**isce**	you understand
lui/lei	cap**isce**	he/she understands
noi	cap**iamo**	we understand
voi	cap**ite**	you understand
loro	cap**iscono**	they understand

Activity B

Write the correct form of each *–ire* verb; 1 and 2 are conjugated like *dormire*, 3 and 4 are conjugated like *capire*.

1 | offrire |    Io _____

2 | aprire |    Lei _____

3 | pulire |    Lui _____

4 | costruire |    Io _____

LESSON 5
Cose da fare

fare la lavatrice

fare i compiti

fare la spesa

fare una telefonata

fare ginnastica

Things to Do

Julia is thinking about the things she has to do today. Look at the pictures and their labels.

Activity A

Choose the correct answer for each question.

1   What is the first thing Julia has to do?
    a   wash clothes   **b   do homework**

2   Which idiomatic expression does not require the article?
    a   fare ginnastica   **b   fare la spesa**

3   Which idiomatic expression means "to do homework"?
    a   fare una telefonata   **b   fare i compiti**

4   What do you think *lavatrice* means?
    a   washing-machine   **b   clothes**

5   What will Julia do after she makes a call?
    a   i compiti   **b   ginnastica**

Cose da fare
fare la lavatrice
fare la spesa
fare i compiti
fare una telefonata
fare ginnastica

SMART TIP

The expression *fare la spesa* (singular, with the article) means to go grocery shopping. In the plural, *fare spese* (or *fare shopping*) means to go shopping.

Activity B

Write the appropriate Italian chore next to each picture.

1 _____

3 _____

Maria
055 26 45 32

2 _____

4 _____

Words to Know

Core Words

I giorni della settimana (Days of the Week)

lunedì	Monday
martedì	Tuesday
mercoledì	Wednesday
giovedì	Thursday
venerdì	Friday
sabato	Saturday
domenica	Sunday

I mesi dell'anno (Months of the Year)

gennaio	January
febbraio	February
marzo	March
aprile	April
maggio	May
giugno	June
luglio	July
agosto	August
settembre	September
ottobre	October
novembre	November
dicembre	December

SMART TIPS

- In Italy, the date is written by placing the day before the month. So November 10 would be 10/11 or *10 novembre*.

- When you want to say that you do something every Monday or Tuesday, for example, you put the article in front of the day of the week. So, *il lunedì* means on Mondays, and so on.

- All years in Italian are expressed as regular numbers. 1999 would be *millenovecentonovantanove* (one thousand nine hundred ninety-nine). 2000 is *duemila* and 2009 is *duemilanove*.

- The names of days and months are not capitalized.

Activity A

Look over Luca's agenda for the week and answer the questions below.

AGENDA

lunedì	fare ginnastica
martedì	fare la spesa
mercoledì	fare i compiti
giovedì	fare ginnastica
venerdì	fare una chiamata negli Stati Uniti
sabato	fare i compiti
domenica	fare la lavatrice

1 What day will Luca go grocery shopping? _____

2 What days will Luca exercise? _____ e _____

3 What day will Luca make a call to the US? _____

4 What days will Luca do his homework? _____ e _____

5 What day will Luca do laundry? _____

Activity B

Write each date in Italian. Remember: The first number is the day.

Example: Thursday 24/02 ____giovedì, 24 febbraio____

1 Monday 17/11 _____

2 Saturday 05/06 _____

3 Wednesday 21/09 _____

4 Friday 08/04 _____

5 Tuesday 31/01 _____

6 Sunday 12/08 _____

7 Thursday 25/03 _____

8 Sunday 14/10 _____

9 Monday 29/05 _____

10 Tuesday 02/12 _____

11 Friday 15/07 _____

12 Wednesday 18/02 _____

LESSON 7

Smart Phrases

Core Phrases

Che giorno è oggi?	What day is today?
(Oggi) è martedì.	Today is Tuesday.
Quanti ne abbiamo oggi?	What is today's date?
(Oggi) è il ___.	Today is ___.
In che mese siamo?	What month is this?
Siamo in ___.	This is _____ (month).
In che anno siamo?	What year is this?
Siamo nel ___.	This is ____ (year).

Activity A

Circle the best response.

1 Che giorno è oggi?
   a gennaio
   b Oggi è martedì.

2 In che mese siamo?
   a lunedì
   b dicembre

3 Quanti ne abbiamo oggi?
   a Oggi è il 14 luglio 2009.
   b Oggi è mercoledì.

4 In che anno siamo?
   a 23 agosto
   b 2009

Activity B

Write the questions to complete the mini-conversations.

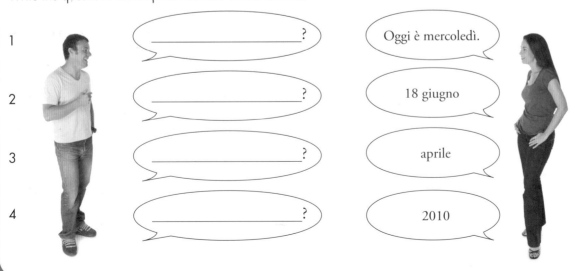

1 _____? — Oggi è mercoledì.

2 _____? — 18 giugno

3 _____? — aprile

4 _____? — 2010

The verb *fare* (to do)

The verb *fare* is irregular. The chart shows its conjugation in the present tense.

io	faccio	I do
tu	fai	you do
Lei	fa	you do
lui/lei	fa	he/she does
noi	facciamo	we do
voi	fate	you do
loro	fanno	they do

Activity A

Fill in the blanks with the correct conjugation of *fare*.

1   Tu _____ i compiti lunedì.

2   Maria _____ una telefonata
    martedì.

3   Io e Luca _____ ginnastica mercoledì.

4   Voi _____ la spesa giovedì.

CULTURE TIPS

The idiomatic expression *fare la lavatrice* means literally "to do the washing-machine." You can also say *fare il bucato* (to do laundry) or *lavare la biancheria* (literally, to wash linen).

Activity B

Che fanno queste persone? Match each picture with a phrase to tell what each person is doing.

1   Lui fa il caffè.   _____

2   Loro fanno conversazione.   _____

3   Lei fa una torta.   _____

4   Io faccio una foto.   _____

5   Loro fanno colazione.   _____

Your Turn

Write sentences telling what activities you do on Saturdays and Sundays. Be sure to use the correct form of the verb *fare*.

_____

_____

_____

_____

_____

_____

_____

Unit 3 Review

Activity A

Choose activities from the box to tell what Irene does at each time. Use the *lei* form of each verb.

> fare i compiti   fare ginnastica   fare la spesa
> fare colazione   fare la lavatrice

1  8:00

Irene fa colazione alle otto.

2  10:00

_____

3  18:00

_____

4  16:00

_____

5 21:30

_____

Activity B

Look at the following times to tell how much time is left in the game.

Example 1:31:02   _Manca un'ora, trentuno minuti e due secondi._

1 2:34:13 _____

2 0:0:27 _____

3 0:12:39 _____

Activity C

Luca lost his planner and forgot his schedule for February. Look at the calendar, then answer the questions.

febbraio						
lunedì	martedì	mercoledì	giovedì	venerdì	sabato	domenica
1	2	3 fare la spesa	4	5	6	7
8	9	10	11	12	13 fare ginnastica	14
15 fare i compiti	16	17	18	19	20	21 fare la lavatrice
22	23 lavare la macchina	24	25	26	27	28

On what dates has Luca scheduled his activities? Write out the date in Italian as day/date/month.

Example go grocery shopping

mercoledì, tre febbraio

1 exercise

_____

2 do homework

_____

3 wash the car

_____

4 do laundry

_____

Internet Activity

Imagine you are in Milan (*Milano*) planning a trip to Rome (*Roma*). Go to **www.berlitzbooks.com/5minute** to browse the site of Alitalia, the Italian airline company. Use your knowledge of dates and time in Italian to search for non-stop flights to Rome. Which flights will get you in on Friday evening? And on Saturday morning?

Challenge

Write a paragraph about a friend. Tell what languages he or she speaks and what he or she usually does during the week.

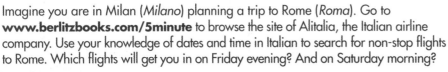

In this unit you will:
- introduce your immediate family and talk about your relatives.
- use possessive adjectives and demonstrative pronouns.
- use indefinite articles.
- learn the irregular verb *avere* (to have).

Patrizia

Paolo

Maurizio e Monica

Carla e i suoi genitori

LESSON 1
Una foto di famiglia

Dialogue

Carla and Alberto are talking about their families. Listen as Carla shows Alberto pictures of her family and tells him who each person is.

Alberto È numerosa la sua famiglia, Carla?

Carla Siamo in sette. Guardi le nostre foto.

Alberto Che bella famiglia! Questa è Lei e questi sono i suoi genitori, vero?

Carla Sì. Lei è mia madre e lui è mio padre. Guardi questa foto. Questa bambina è mia sorella, Patrizia.

Alberto E questi sono i suoi fratelli?

Carla Sì. Questo è mio fratello Maurizio. Lui è il maggiore. E questo è Paolo, il mio fratello minore.

Alberto Chi è questa signora?

Carla Lei è Monica, la moglie di Maurizio.

Activity A

Circle **T** for true or **F** for false.

1 There are fewer than five people in Carla's family.   T/F
2 Patrizia is Carla's sister.   T/F
3 Carla has three brothers.   T/F
4 Monica is Carla's mother.   T/F

Activity B

Read the following phrases. Circle the picture that illustrates each phrase.

1 Questo è mio padre.   a   b

2 Questa è mia sorella.   a   b

3 Questa è mia madre.   a   b

4 Questi sono i miei fratelli. a   b

5 Questa è la moglie di Maurizio.   a   b

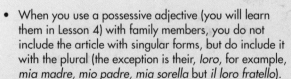

SMART TIPS

- When you use a possessive adjective (you will learn them in Lesson 4) with family members, you do not include the article with singular forms, but do include it with the plural (the exception is their, *loro*, for example, *mia madre, mio padre, mia sorella* but *il loro fratello*).

- Other words for *padre* and *madre* are *papà* (or *babbo*, used in the Tuscany region) and *mamma*. In these cases the article is used in front of the possessive adjective: *il mio papà, la mia mamma*. The article is also used with modified singular family members (*il mio fratello maggiore*) or with terms of endearment: *il tuo fratellino* (your little brother), *la sua sorellina* (his/her little sister).

Words to Know

Core Words

la famiglia	family
il marito	husband
la moglie	wife
i genitori	parents
la madre	mother
il padre	father
la figlia	daughter
il figlio	son
i figli	children
il fratello	brother
la sorella	sister
i fratelli	brothers/siblings

Extra Words

il maggiore	oldest
il minore	youngest

Alberto's Family Tree

Tommaso   Marina

Alberto   Giulia   Marco

SMART TIPS

There are two ways to talk about possession:

- by using possessive adjectives such as *il mio* (my). You will learn these adjectives in Lesson 4.
- by using the definite article + noun (possession) + *di*. For example: *il marito di Maria* (Maria's husband).

Activity A

Look at Alberto's family tree. Complete his description. The first one is done for you.

Siamo in cinque nella mia ___famiglia___ . Tommaso
                                    family

è mio _____ . Mia _____
         father   mother

si chiama Marina. Giulia è mia _____ .
                                        sister

Marco è il _____ di Giulia.
                husband

Activity B

Circle the correct word.

1 Alberto e Giulia sono **fratelli   genitori**.

2 Alberto è il **fratello   padre**   di Giulia.

3 Marina è la **sorella   madre**   di Alberto.

4 Tommaso è il **figlio   padre**   di Alberto e Giulia.

5 Marina e Tommaso sono i **figli   genitori** di Alberto e Giulia.

6 Alberto è il **marito   figlio**   di Marina e Tommaso.

7 Giulia è la **figlia   figlio**   di Marina e Tommaso.

8 Alberto e Giulia sono i **figli   genitori** di Marina e Tommaso.

9 Giulia è la **moglie   sorella**   di Marco.

10 Marco è il **marito   fratello**   di Giulia.

Core Phrases

È numerosa la sua famiglia?	How big is your family?
(In famiglia) siamo in _____.	There are _____ of us (in the family).
La mia famiglia è numerosa/poco numerosa.	My family is big/small.
Che bella famiglia!	What a nice family!
Che famiglia numerosa/poco numerosa!	What a big/small family!

Activity A

Put the phrases in order to create a dialogue.

È numerosa la sua famiglia?

#1

No. La mia famiglia è poco numerosa. Siamo in quattro.

#

Sì, la mia famiglia è numerosa. E la sua famiglia è numerosa?

#

Che famiglia numerosa!

#

Nella mia famiglia siamo in otto. Guardi questa foto.

#

#

Activity B

Write a phrase to tell whether each family is big or small.

1 _____

2 _____

3 _____

4 _____

Your Turn

Use your new vocabulary and phrases to talk about your family. Is it big or small? Do you have any siblings? How many?

	Singular (m/f)	Plural (m/f)
before a consonant	questo/questa (this) quel/quella (that)	questi/queste (these) quei/quelle (those)
before s+ consonant, z, ps, gn	quello/quella	quegli/quelle
before a vowel	quell'	quegli/quelle

Note that *questo/questa* can become *quest'* in front of a singular noun beginning with a vowel. And, *quello/quella/quelli/quelle* follow the same definite article rules when in front of a noun (see Unit 2, p. 20).

Activity B

Read the sentences below. Write the letter of the corresponding picture next to each sentence.

1 Queste bambine sono le mie figlie. _____

2 Quella macchina è di mia sorella. _____

3 Quest'uomo è mio padre. _____

4 Quella casa è di mio fratello. _____

5 Questa donna è mia madre. _____

6 Queste persone sono i miei genitori. _____

7 Quei cani sono di mio fratello. _____

8 Questi bambini sono i miei figli. _____

Possessive Adjectives

Possessive adjectives always agree in gender and number with the noun to which they refer and are preceded by a definite article. Remember, though, to drop the article in front of singular family members (see Smart Tips on p. 35).

Singular (m/f)	Plural (m/f)	English
il mio/la mia	i miei/le mie	my
il tuo/la tua	i tuoi/le tue	your (sing., inf.)
il suo/la sua	i suoi/le sue	his/her/its, your (sing., form.)
il nostro/la nostra	i nostri/le nostre	our
il vostro/la vostra	i vostri/le vostre	your (pl.)
il loro/la loro	i loro/le loro	their

Activity A

Fill in the blanks with the correct possessive adjectives. They may be either singular or plural, feminine or masculine, depending on the gender of the noun.

1 Lei è _____ madre. (my)

2 È _____ macchina? (your, inf.)

3 _____ famiglia è poco numerosa. (your, form.)

4 Loro sono _____ sorelle. (my)

5 Sono loro _____ genitori? (your, inf.)

6 Loro sono _____ fratelli. (your, form.)

7 _____ casa è bella. (our)

8 I bambini sono _____ figli. (our)

Demonstrative Adjectives

Demonstrative adjectives agree in gender and number with the noun to which they refer. *Quello/quella/quelli/quelle* follow the same rules of the definite article when in front of a noun (see Unit 2, p. 20).

L'albero genealogico

Ada
(nonna)

Giovanni
(nonno)

Family Tree

Paola Rossi has just created a family tree for her records. Look at the tree and read each relationship aloud.

Roberta
(zia)

Lorenzo
(zio)

Lucia
(madre)

Carlo
(padre)

Activity A

Describe the relationship of each person to Paola.

1 Giovanni is _____

2 Lucia is _____

3 Adele is _____

4 Linda is _____

Giuseppe
(cugino)

Adele
(cugina)

Paola

Luca
(fratello)

Nadia
(cognata)

Activity B

Can you tell who's who in Paola's family? Write the relationship of each person beside his or her picture.

Giacomo
(nipote)

Linda
(nipote)

1  _____

2  _____

3   _____

4 _____

SMART TIPS

- In the plural, both the masculine and feminine forms of *nipote* are *nipoti*: *i nipoti, le nipoti*. Also be careful with the word *i parenti*, which means relatives (not parents).

- *Il nipote* means both nephew and grandson and *la nipote* means both niece and granddaughter.

- In Italian *il suo/la sua, i suoi/le sue* agree in gender and number with the noun they modify and not with the person who owns it: Maria and her dog will be *Maria e il suo cane* (m), Maurizio and his house will be *Maurizio e la sua casa* (f).

Words to Know

Core Words

il cugino	cousin (m)
la cugina	cousin (f)
il nipote	nephew/grandson
la nipote	niece/granddaughter
il nonno	grandfather
la nonna	grandmother
lo zio	uncle
la zia	aunt

Extra Words

il cognato	brother-in-law
la cognata	sister-in-law
il genero	son-in-law
la nuora	daughter-in-law
il suocero	father-in-law
la suocera	mother-in-law

Activity A

Match the Italian word with its English equivalent.

> zia   nuora   cugina   nipote   nonni   nonno

1   cousin (f) _____

2   nephew _____

3   aunt _____

4   daughter-in-law _____

5   grandfather _____

6   grandparents _____

Activity B

How are you related? Complete the statements by circling the correct relative.

1   La sorella di mia madre è mia…

   a zia   **b nipote**

2   Il figlio di mia zia è mio…

   a cugino   **b cugina**

3   La madre di mio padre è mia…

   a nonno   **b nonna**

4   Il cugino di mio figlio è mio…

   a nipote   **b cognato**

5   Il padre di mio padre è mio…

   a nonno   **b zio**

6   La nipote di mio padre è mia…

   a cugino   **b cugina**

SMART TIP

You can add the suffix *–astro* or *–astra* to the names of some step-family members: *fratellastro, sorellastra, figliastro/figliastra*. However, many Italians avoid using them because *-astro* has a negative connotation. So, for example, for *fratellastro* they might use *figlio di mio padre* (my father's son), for *figliastra* they might use *figlia di mio marito/moglie* (daughter of my husband/wife).

LESSON 7

Smart Phrases

Core Phrases

Ha parenti?	Do you have any relatives?
È unita la sua famiglia?	Is your family close?
Ho una famiglia unita.	My family is close.
È sposato/sposata?	Are you married (m/f)?
Sono celibe/nubile.	I'm single (m/f).
Voglio bene alla mia famiglia.	I love my family.
Ti amo.	I love you.

Activity A

Draw a line to match the questions and statements with the correct response.

1 È molto unita la sua famiglia?   No, sono sposata. Quello è mio marito.

2 Suo fratello è molto bello! È sposato?   Sì, la mia famiglia è molto unita.

3 Ha parenti?   No, è celibe.

4 È nubile?   Sì, ho una famiglia numerosa.

SMART TIP

Ti voglio bene is normally used to express love to family members and friends while *Ti amo* is reserved for romantic partners. Remember that the informal "you" is used in each phrase.

Ti amo.

Activity B

What do you say if you want to...

1 ...tell your husband/wife that you love him/her?

_____

2 ...tell your mother that you love her?

_____

3 ...tell someone that your family is close?

_____

4 ...ask someone if he/she is married?

_____

CULTURE TIP

In everyday Italian the expression *Sono single* is very common for *Sono celibe/nubile.*

Your Turn

Now talk about you and your relatives. Are you single or married? Who is married in your family? Who is single?

LESSON 8

Smart Grammar

Indefinite Articles (a/an)

The indefinite article in Italian follows the rule of the definite article (see p. 20). Each is used according to the first letter or two letters (s + consonant, gn, ps) of the noun that follows.

M	F
un in front of a vowel and consonant	**un'** in front of a feminine noun starting with a vowel
uno in front of z, s + consonant, gn, ps	**una** in front of all consonants

Activity A

Write the correct indefinite article and noun next to each picture.

1 _____

2 _____

3 _____

4 _____

The verb *avere* (to have)

The verb *avere* is irregular. Look at the chart for its conjugation in the present tense.

io	ho	I have
tu	hai	you have
Lei	ha	you have
lui/lei	ha	he/she has
noi	abbiamo	we have
voi	avete	you have
loro	hanno	they have

Examples

Lui ha una cugina. He has a cousin.
Noi abbiamo uno zio. We have an uncle.

Activity B

Write a sentence using the correct form of *avere*.

1 tu, fratello _____

2 io, cugino _____

3 loro, zia _____

4 voi, nipote _____

Your Turn

Answer the following questions about your family.

1 Ha zii? _____

2 Ha nipoti? _____

3 Hanno figli i suoi zii? _____

4 Hanno figli i suoi cugini? _____

SMART TIP

The verb *avere* is sometimes used as the equivalent of the verb "to be." If you want to say "I'm hungry," you would say *Ho fame*, which literally means "I have hunger." "I'm thirsty" is *Ho sete*, and "I'm cold" is *Ho freddo*. Can you tell the equivalent of "I'm hot *(caldo)*"?

Activity A

The Bianchi family is having a *festa* (party) for *nonno* Alfonso. Serena has brought her new boyfriend Carlo and is pointing out family members to him. Complete Serena and Carlo's conversation about her family.

Serena Questo è mio _____, Alfonso.
  grandfather

E questa è mia _____, Giulia.
  grandmother

Carlo Chi è questa signora?

Serena Lei è mia _____, Laura, e questo è suo
  cousin

_____, Giuseppe.
  brother

Carlo È tua _____ quella signora?
  mother

Serena No, quella è mia _____, Sara.
  aunt

Laura e Giuseppe sono i suoi _____.
  children

Carlo È questa tua madre?

Serena No, questa è mia _____ Linda,
  aunt

_____ di mio _____ Giovanni.
  the wife   uncle

Lui è _____ di mio _____.
  the brother   father

Carlo La tua _____ è numerosa. E dov'è
  family

tua madre?

Serena I miei _____ non sono alla festa.
  parents

Activity B

Tell how each person is related to Serena. Use the correct possessive adjective before the person's title.

Example Alfonso è suo nonno.

1 Giulia _____

2 Laura e Giuseppe _____

3 Sara e Linda _____

4 Giovanni _____

Activity C

At the party, Giovanni asks Carlo questions about his family. Fill in the dialogue with Carlo's responses.

Giovanni La sua famiglia è numerosa o poco numerosa?

  Carlo _____

Giovanni Ha fratelli?

  Carlo _____

Giovanni Ha zii?

  Carlo _____

Activity D

Now Carlo is asking Alfonso about his family. Fill in the blanks with the correct demonstrative adjectives.

Carlo _____ bambino è suo nipote?
  That

Alfonso No, _____ bambino è mio nipote.
  this

Carlo _____ signora è sua moglie?
  That

Alfonso No, _____ signora è mia moglie.
  this

Carlo _____ ragazze sono le sue figlie?
  Those

Alfonso No, _____ ragazze sono le mie figlie.
  these

Activity E

Write a sentence telling how many children each family has.

1

_____

2

_____

3

_____

4

_____

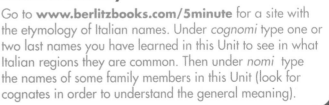

Internet Activity

Go to **www.berlitzbooks.com/5minute** for a site with the etymology of Italian names. Under *cognomi* type one or two last names you have learned in this Unit to see in what Italian regions they are common. Then under *nomi* type the names of some family members in this Unit (look for cognates in order to understand the general meaning).

Unit 5   Meals

In this unit you will:
- discuss *la colazione* (breakfast), *il pranzo* (lunch) and *la cena* (dinner).
- use food and drink vocabulary.
- form questions in Italian.
- use the irregular verb *volere* (to want).

LESSON 1

Ho fame!

Dialogue

Maria and Sergio talk about what they want to eat. Listen as they discuss food for *la colazione*, *il pranzo* and *la cena*. Note that as friends, Maria and Sergio address each other informally.

Maria   Ho fame. Facciamo colazione?

Sergio   Sì, ho voglia di un'insalata.

Maria   Alle otto di mattina? L'insalata si mangia a pranzo o a cena.

Sergio   Va bene. Che cosa vuoi mangiare?

Maria   Delle uova. Ti va di fare una colazione all'inglese?

Sergio   Sì, però ho voglia di bere del vino.

Maria   Ma il vino non si beve a colazione!

Activity A

Circle **T** for true and **F** for false.

1   Maria wants to eat breakfast.   T/F
2   Sergio wants to eat salad for breakfast.   T/F
3   Maria tells Sergio that they should eat soup.   T/F
4   Sergio is in the mood for a beer.   T/F

Activity B

Circle the correct answer.

1   What does Maria want to eat?
    a   b

2   What is Sergio in the mood to drink?
    a    b

3   What are they going to eat for breakfast?
    a   b

4   What time does the dialogue take place?
    a   b

SMART TIP

The preposition *di* has several meanings, including:
- of (belonging)
- of (made of) quantity (*un po' di*)
- from

It is also used after some expressions (*Ho voglia di un'insalata*).

In order to express a quantity (some) use *di* + the definite article (used always in affirmative sentences). Note the following contractions and change of spelling (*di* becomes *de*):
- di + il = del
- di + lo = dello
- di + la = della
- di + l' = dell'
- di + i = dei
- di + gli = degli
- di + le = delle

LESSON 2
Words to Know

Core Words

Il cibo (Food)

la frutta	fruit
il pane	bread
la pasta	pasta
l'uovo	egg
la zuppa	soup

Le bevande (Drinks)

l'acqua	water
la birra	beer
il caffè	coffee
il latte	milk
il succo	juice
il tè	tea
il vino	wine

Food Verbs

bere	to drink
mangiare	to eat
prendere	to take/eat/drink

CULTURE TIPS

Pizza is perhaps the most famous and popular Italian food all over the world. There are different types of pizza and its thickness can vary in different regions. In Italy the well-known pizza from Naples is usually thicker and its uniqueness is due to different factors: secret ingredients that make the dough taste different, baking it in a wood-burning oven and the use of buffalo mozzarella.

SMART TIP

The word *uovo* (egg) is irregular in the plural. Pay attention to the article: *le uova*.

Activity A

Look at the pictures and write, in Italian, the food or drink that each person enjoys.

1 _____   2 _____

3 _____   4 _____

Activity B

Use the word box below to tell what you eat and drink for breakfast, lunch and dinner. Be sure to use the conjunction *e* (and).

> della frutta   del pane   del vino
> della pasta   dell'acqua   del caffè

1 colazione _____

2 pranzo _____

3 cena _____

SMART TIP

Think of *prendere* as the Italian equivalent of "to have" in regards to food and drink. If you want to say that you can't have coffee, say *Non posso prendere il caffè*.

LESSON 3

Smart Phrases

Core Phrases

Ho fame.	I'm hungry.
Ho sete.	I'm thirsty.
Ho voglia di bere ___.	I'm in the mood to drink ___.
Ho voglia di mangiare ___.	I'm in the mood to eat ___.
Facciamo colazione!	Let's have breakfast!
Pranziamo!	Let's have lunch!
Ceniamo!	Let's have dinner!
Vorrei...	I would like...

> **SMART TIP**
>
> The nouns *pranzo* and *cena* can be made into verbs by dropping the final vowel and adding the ending *–are*. This means that *pranzo* is the meal while *pranzare* is the action. Note that this does not apply to *colazione*: to have breakfast is *fare colazione*.

Activity A

Six people want different things to eat or drink. Read the items on the left and decide if the person is hungry or thirsty. Check the appropriate answer.

		Ho fame.	**Ho sete.**
1	pane e frutta	☐	☐
2	latte e tè	☐	☐
3	zuppa e insalata	☐	☐
4	birra e acqua	☐	☐
5	uova	☐	☐
6	succo	☐	☐

Activity B

Fill in the blanks with the correct Italian phrase.

1 _____ un'insalata.
           I'm in the mood to eat

2 _____ una birra.
           I'm in the mood to drink

Activity C

Write the correct Italian phrase.

1   Let's have breakfast!

2   Let's have lunch!

3   Let's have dinner!

LESSON 4
Smart Grammar

Question Words

Che cosa?	What?
Chi?	Who?
Come?	How?
Come mai?	How come?
Dove?	Where?
Perché?	Why?
Quale?	Which one?
Quali?	Which ones?
Quando?	When?
Quanto/Quanta?	How much? (m/f)
Quanti/Quante?	How many? (m/f)

SMART TIPS

• To begin an open-ended question, start with a question word and then use a conjugated verb.

Examples:

Chi è il suo amico?	Who is your friend?
Quando mangiamo?	When do we eat?
Com'è la sua famiglia?	What's your family like?
Che cosa mangia a pranzo?	What do you eat for lunch?

• Note that *quale/quali* and *quanto/quanta/quanti/quante* agree in gender and number with the noun they modify.

Examples:

Quale birra vuoi?	Which beer do you want?
Quante pizze vuoi?	How many pizzas do you want?

• *Come* and *dove* elide in front of the verb *essere*: *Com'è? Dov'è?*

Quale just drops the final vowel: *Qual è?*

• *Che, Che cosa* and *cosa* are used interchangeably. But with time you just use *che*:

Che ore sono?	What time is it?

Activity A

Fill in the blanks with the correct question word. Choose the word from the word box.

> Che cosa   Dove   Qual   Quando

1 _____ abita?

2 _____ è il suo indirizzo?

3 _____ prende? Una birra, grazie.

4 _____ va al cinema?

Activity B

Ask questions using the following question words.

1 Quali _____?

2 Come mai _____?

3 Perché _____?

4 Chi _____?

5 Quanti _____?

Activity C

What question word do you use to ask…

1 …for a reason?

_____

2 …who someone is?

_____

3 …when an event is going to happen?

_____

4 …which object someone is pointing to?

_____

5 …where someone lives?

_____

Your Turn

Read the following answers. Then ask a question for each answer. Practice this in front of a mirror. Saying the questions and answers aloud and watching how your mouth moves will help your pronunciation.

1 Mia madre si chiama Giulia.

2 Abito a Roma.

3 Quelli sono i cugini di Marco.

4 Sono le otto.

Al ristorante

Menu

Read the menu aloud. Next, listen to the dialogue. Marta talks to *il cameriere* (the waiter) about what she will order at the restaurant.

Ristorante La veranda

Antipasti
Prosciutto e melone
Antipasto di mare
Bruschette

Primi piatti
Risotto ai funghi
Spaghetti al pomodoro
Lasagne

Secondi piatti
Pollo arrosto
Pesce alla griglia

Contorni
Insalata mista
Verdure al vapore
Patate al forno

Dolci
Tiramisù
Torta al cioccolato
Gelato

Dialogue

Cameriere	Buon giorno, che cosa desidera?
Marta	Vorrei un antipasto, che cosa mi consiglia?
Cameriere	L'antipasto di mare è molto buono.
Marta	Va bene. Non voglio un primo però, ma vorrei il secondo. Prendo il pollo arrosto.
Cameriere	Vuole un contorno?
Marta	Sì, prendo l'insalata mista.
Cameriere	E da bere?
Marta	Vorrei dell'acqua, grazie.
Cameriere	Desidera altro?
Marta	No, grazie.

Activity A

Circle the correct picture based on the dialogue and the menu.

1   What does Marta want for her appetizer?

2   What does Marta want for her second course?

3   What does Marta have as a side dish?

4   What is an option for dessert on the menu?

Activity B

Number the phrases 1–4 to create a dialogue.

____   Vorrei un secondo.

____   Vuole anche un contorno?

____   Buon giorno, che cosa desidera?

____   Sì, prendo l'insalata mista.

CULTURE TIP

Italians usually eat *un primo (piatto)* (a first course) consisting of *pasta* or *riso* or *zuppa, un secondo (piatto)* (a second course) consisting of *carne* or *pesce,* and *un contorno* (a side dish) consisting of vegetables. Note that *l'insalata* is not served at the beginning of a meal since it is considered a side dish. Italians have a three-course meal during the weekends, or at lunch if they do not work or do not need to go back to work. Otherwise, they just eat *un panino* (a sandwich) or a light lunch. For special occasions they usually start a meal with *un antipasto* (appetizer) and finish with *un dolce* (dessert).

Words to Know

Altre parole sul cibo (More Words on Food)

la bistecca	steak
la carne	meat
il formaggio	cheese
il gelato	ice cream
l'insalata	salad
le patate	potatoes
il pesce	fish
il pollo	chicken
il riso	rice
la torta	cake
le verdure	vegetables

Activity A

Decide whether each set of food items is an appetizer, a first or second course, a side dish or a dessert. On the lines provided, write *antipasto, primo (piatto), secondo (piatto), contorno* or *dolce*.

1   il riso e la pasta _____

2   la carne e il pesce _____

3   il gelato e la torta _____

4   l'insalata e le verdure _____

5   la bruschetta e il prosciutto e melone _____

CULTURE TIP

In Italy, *il servizio* (service) is usually included in the bill so it is not necessary to leave a tip. However, you can leave a small tip on the table for excellent service.

Activity B

Use the menu on page 48 to answer the following questions in Italian. Be sure to write complete sentences.

1   Qual è un antipasto?

_____

2   Qual è un secondo piatto?

_____

3   Qual è un dolce?

_____

Your Turn

Use your new vocabulary and phrases to create your own menu.

Ristorante _____
Menu

Antipasti	Contorni
_____	_____
_____	_____
Primi piatti	Dolci
_____	_____
_____	_____
Secondi piatti	Bevande
_____	_____
_____	_____

Smart Phrases

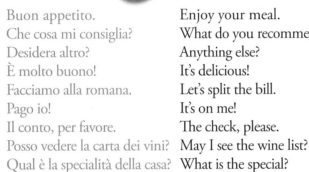

Core Phrases

Buon appetito.	Enjoy your meal.
Che cosa mi consiglia?	What do you recommend?
Desidera altro?	Anything else?
È molto buono!	It's delicious!
Facciamo alla romana.	Let's split the bill.
Pago io!	It's on me!
Il conto, per favore.	The check, please.
Posso vedere la carta dei vini?	May I see the wine list?
Qual è la specialità della casa?	What is the special?
La specialità è _____.	The special is _____.

Activity A

What do you say if you want to…

1   …tell someone to enjoy his/her meal?

_____

2   …ask the waiter for the check?

_____

3   …say that something tastes delicious?

_____

4   …ask for the wine list?

_____

CULTURE TIPS

- In Italy *un ristorante* is a formal place and can be expensive. If you want to spend less money and eat in an informal environment, then choose *una trattoria*, usually a family-run business. Finally, choose *una pizzeria* if you're in the mood for a pizza.

- An Italian *bar* (café) is different from an American one. It is very common to stop by in the morning for a coffee or to have breakfast with a *cornetto* (brioche) or *cappuccino*. Usually people drink or eat standing at the counter.

Activity B

Circle the best response to the questions and scenarios below.

1   Qual è la specialità della casa?

   a   **È molto buono!**

   b   **La specialità è il pesce.**

2   It is the beginning of the meal and you want something to drink. You say to *al cameriere*:

   a   **Posso vedere la carta dei vini?**

   b   **Buon appetito.**

3   You are eating and the waiter wants to know if you like the food. You answer:

   a   **La specialità è la carne.**

   b   **È molto buono!**

4   It is the end of the meal. You say to *al cameriere:*

   a   **Il conto, per favore.**

   b   **Qual è la specialità della casa?**

Your Turn

You are at a restaurant with a friend. Tell him about the food, the menu and the specials. Ask him about his food. At the end, be polite and take care of the check.

The verb *volere* (to want)

The verb *volere* is irregular. The chart shows its conjugation in the present tense.

io	voglio	I want
tu	vuoi	you want
Lei	vuole	you want
lui/lei	vuole	he/she wants
noi	vogliamo	we want
voi	volete	you want
loro	vogliono	they want

SMART TIPS

- Use *vorrei* (I would like) when ordering something at a restaurant; it's a more polite way of asking for things.

- Use the verb *preferire* (to prefer) if you want to say what you prefer: *Preferisco il pollo* (I prefer chicken). Remember that *preferire* belongs to the verbs in *-ire* that add *-isc* (See Unit 3 p. 29).

- Add *non* before the appropriate conjugation of *volere* to indicate the negative form of the verb. For example, *Non voglio il dolce* (I don't want dessert).

Activity A

Write the correct form of the verb *volere* to complete the phrases.

1 Lei non _____ il pollo come secondo.

2 Noi _____ l'insalata come contorno.

3 Loro _____ il gelato come dolce.

4 Anna, _____ il risotto?

Activity B

What do you want to eat? Complete the sentences below with the *io* form of *volere* to explain what you do and do not want to eat.

1 _____ _____ come secondo.
   I want   chicken

2 _____ _____ come antipasto.
   I don't want   cheese

3 _____ _____ come secondo.
   I want   fish

4 _____ _____ come primo.
   I don't want   pasta

5 _____ _____ come dolce.
   I want   cake

6 _____ _____ come contorno.
   I don't want   vegetables

Your Turn

Vuole carne o verdure? Say out loud which food items you want to eat. Then use *preferire* to say which food items you prefer.

l'insalata

il pesce

il pollo

le patate

Unit 5 Review

Activity A

Look at the pictures, then write complete sentences to say what people want for lunch and what they prefer for dinner. Use the personal pronouns *io, tu, lui/lei, noi, voi* and *loro*. One sentence has been done for you.

A pranzo (volere)

1 Voglio mangiare una zuppa e bere dell'acqua.
2 _____
3 _____
4 _____
5 _____
6 _____

A cena (preferire)

1 _____
2 _____
3 _____
4 _____
5 _____
6 Preferiscono mangiare la carne e bere una birra.

Activity B

There's a problem with the menu at la Trattoria Italia. Someone mixed up appetizers, first and second courses and desserts. Cross out the mistakes and replace them with the correct words.

Trattoria Italia

Menu

Antipasti
Tiramisù
Bruschetta

Primi
Pollo arrosto
Torta al cioccolato

Secondi
Risotto ai funghi
Pesce alla griglia

Dolci
Carne arrosto

Activity C

Mario is hungry, so he and Lucia go out to dinner. Use the phrases and question words you learned in this unit to fill in the blanks of their dialogue.

Mario _____ fame.

Lucia _____ vuoi mangiare?

Mario _____ del pesce.

Lucia Andiamo _____.

In the car

Mario _____ è il ristorante?

Lucia È là. (Points to a restaurant down the block.)

At the restaurant before eating

Lucia Che _____ come primo?

Mario Vorrei _____.

At the restaurant after eating

Lucia Cameriere, _____, per favore.

Challenge

Look at the word *melagrana*. What do you think it means? (Hint: It's a type of fruit.) After you take a guess at its meaning, look up the word in an Italian-English dictionary to see if you're right. Then look up other kinds of fruit to further expand your vocabulary. Repeat the activity with other food items as well. Visit **www.berlitzbooks.com/5minute** for a list of online dictionaries.

Internet Activity

Go to **www.berlitzbooks.com/5minute** for a list of sites of Italian restaurants to browse. Look for a menu and read it out loud. *Quali sono gli antipasti? I primi piatti? E i secondi?* If you don't know what certain words mean, write them down and look them up.

Weather and Temperature

In this unit, you will:
- talk about temperature, weather and seasons.
- learn about qualitative adjectives.
- learn the present progressive tense.

 LESSON 1

Che tempo fa?

Dialogue

Carlo lives in Palermo and Fernanda lives in Milan. Listen to their phone conversation about the weather in their cities.

Carlo Buon giorno Fernanda! Che tempo fa a Milano?

Fernanda Fa freddo. C'è il sole, però ci sono dieci gradi.

Carlo Davvero? Anche a Palermo fa brutto tempo.

Fernanda Qual è la temperatura?

Carlo Ci sono venticinque gradi e piove.

Fernanda Venticinque gradi? Ma non è brutto!

Activity A

Match the questions with the correct picture.

1 Che tempo fa a Milano?

2 Che tempo fa a Palermo?

3 Qual è la temperatura a Milano?

4 Qual è la temperatura a Palermo?

Activity B

Reread the dialogue and look for words to complete the crossword below. Three out of the five words are cognates (words that are similar in Italian and English).

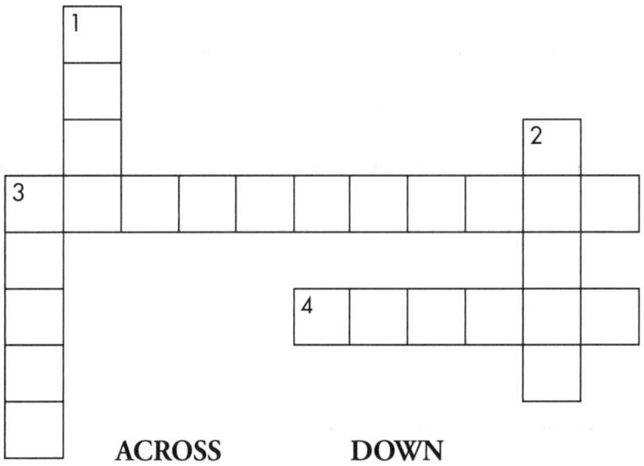

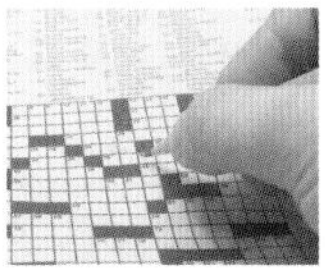

[crossword grid]

ACROSS
3 temperature
4 cold

DOWN
1 sun
2 degree
3 weather

SMART TIP

The word *anche* means "also" and "too." It is used at the beginning of a sentence to stress a contrast. For example:

Anche a Palermo fa freddo. — It's also cold in Palermo.
Anche lei sente freddo. — She is cold too.

Words to Know

CULTURE TIP

In Italy, *la temperatura* (temperature) is measured in *gradi Celsius* or *gradi (centigradi)* (Celsius or centigrade). The most common term is *gradi*.

To convert Fahrenheit to Celsius, use this formula:

$C = (F - 32) \div 1.8$

And Celsius to Fahrenheit:

$F = (1.8 \times C) + 32$

Core Words

caldo	hot
freddo	cold
la neve	snow
nuvoloso	cloudy
la pioggia	rain
piovoso	rainy
il sole	sun
il tempo	weather
umido	humid
il vento	wind

Activity A

Use the vocabulary to complete the dialogue.

Che _____ fa in Svizzera?
　　　　weather

Fa _____ e _____.
　　cold　　　　it's cloudy

Qual è _____?
　　　　the temperature

Ci sono dieci _____.
　　　　　degrees

Davvero? Qui fa _____.
　　　　　hot
_____.
It's humid.

Activity B

Circle the appropriate word or phrase to complete each thought.

1 It's a nice day.

　a Ci sono trenta gradi.　　**b Fa freddo.**

2 It's 2 degrees Celsius.

　a Fa caldo.　　**b Fa freddo.**

3 It's raining and it's windy. This describes:

　a la temperatura　　**b il tempo**

4 It's 6 degrees Celsius outside. This is:

　a il tempo　　**b la temperatura**

Activity C

Match the appropriate word to each picture.

1　nuvoloso　　　**a**

2　piovoso　　　**b**

3　il vento　　　**c**

4　il sole　　　**d**

Smart Phrases

Che tempo fa? Match each picture with the best description of the weather.

1    **a** Fa caldo.

Core Phrases

Che tempo fa?	What's the weather like?
C'è il sole.	It's sunny.
C'è vento.	It's windy.
Ci sono_____ gradi.	It's _____ degrees.
Fa bel/brutto tempo.	The weather is nice/bad.
Fa caldo/freddo.	It's hot/cold.

2    **b** C'è il sole.

Extra Phrases

Sta nevicando.	It's snowing.
Sta piovendo.	It's raining.

3    **c** Fa brutto tempo.

CULTURE TIP

If someone is talking about the weather and you hear *piove a catinelle,* you better bring your *ombrello* (umbrella). Literally meaning "It's raining buckets," it is the equivalent to the English expression "It's raining cats and dogs."

4    **d** Fa freddo.

Activity A

Write each word or phrase in the appropriate column.

35°C	Fa caldo.	6°C
Fa bel tempo.	32°F	Fa freddo.

Qual è la temperatura?	Che tempo fa?
_____	_____
_____	_____
_____	_____

Activity C

Imagine it is a warm spring day. Read the questions and circle the appropriate answers.

1 Che tempo fa?

   a Fa bel tempo.   **b** Fa brutto tempo.

2 Fa caldo o freddo?

   a Fa caldo.   **b** Fa freddo.

3 Qual è la temperatura?

   a Ci sono cinque gradi.   **b** Ci sono ventisei gradi.

Adjective Placement

In Italian, most adjectives come after the noun. Some, however, come before the noun, while others vary depending on their meaning. Here are a few rules to remember:

- After the noun = color, shape, religion, nationality.

Examples

un tè verde	a green tea
un piatto rotondo	a round plate
una chiesa cattolica	a Catholic church
una ragazza svizzera	a Swiss girl

- Before the noun = adjectives following the acronym BAGS (beauty, age, good/bad, size).

Examples

la bella ragazza	the beautiful girl
il giovane ragazzo	the young guy
il bravo studente	the good student
il piccolo cane	the little dog

- Some adjectives change meaning depending on their placement. The chart shows some common examples:

Italian adjective	Meaning before the noun	Meaning after the noun
bravo/a (m/f)	good	really good
certo/a (m/f)	particular	evident
caro/a (m/f)	dear	expensive
grande	famous	tall
povero/a (m/f)	poor (pitiful)	poor (not rich)
nuovo/a (m/f)	another	new

Activity A

Write the adjective in the correct place in the phrase.

1 la _____ ragazza _____ (bella)
2 il _____ cane _____ (piccolo)
3 la _____ macchina _____ (rossa)
4 il _____ ragazzo _____ (americano)
5 la _____ tavola_____ (rotonda)

Activity B

Choose the correct meaning of the adjective based on its location in the phrase.

1 una macchina nuova
   a a new car   **b another car**

2 l'uomo povero
   a the poor (not rich) man   **b the pitiful man**

3 una grande donna
   a a tall woman   **b a famous woman**

4 un uomo bravo
   a a good man   **b a really good man**

SMART TIP

Another adjective that changes place depending on its meaning is *vecchio/a*. When placed before the noun it means "known for a long time." For example: *È un vecchio amico* means "He is a friend I have known for many years." When placed after the noun it means "old." For example: *Un amico vecchio* "An elderly friend."

Your Turn

Now think of some other common adjectives. Look them up in an Italian-English Dictionary and use the rules to decide where to place them.

LESSON 5

Che sta facendo?

What are you doing? Read this fact sheet and *l'intervista* (interview) with Antonio Bianchi, a famous soccer player. Take a look to see what Antonio likes to do and wear for each season.

Nome Antonio Bianchi
Età 33 anni
Nazionalità Italiana
Occupazione Calciatore
Attività preferite
correre giocare a calcio viaggiare nuotare

Intervista

Giornalista	Che fa di solito in estate?
Antonio	In estate gioco a calcio, nuoto e corro.
Giornalista	Viaggia durante l'estate?
Antonio	No, viaggiare in estate è noioso. In estate sto in Italia, ma in inverno viaggio un po' nei paesi del Nord Europa.
Giornalista	In estate non ha bisogno di molti vestiti: bastano pantaloncini, magliette e un costume. Però in inverno...
Antonio	Ha ragione. In inverno fa freddo nei paesi del Nord Europa. Porto il cappotto, i guanti e la sciarpa.
Giornalista	Ho una sua foto. Dov'è in questa foto?
Antonio	Sono a Roma.

Activity A

Complete the word web with the activities Antonio does in the summer.

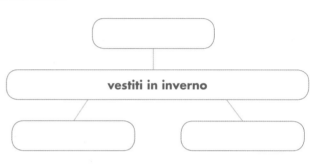

Complete the word web with the clothing Antonio wears in the winter.

Activity B

Complete the following sentences about Antonio.

1 Antonio swims, runs and _____ in the summer.

2 Antonio travels in the _____.

3 Antonio wears a coat in the _____.

4 Antonio is from _____ and is _____ years old.

CULTURE TIP

According to a recent poll, *il calcio* (soccer) is still the most popular sport in Italy but not the most practiced anymore. Italians prefer aerobics, fitness and body building to soccer. Dance is also becoming more and more popular with over a million people choosing it as a sport or a hobby.

LESSON 6

Smart Phrases

Core Phrases

Che fa di solito?	What do you usually do?
Che sta facendo?	What are you doing?
Durante l'estate io di solito_____.	In the summer, I usually_____.
È divertente.	It's fun.
È noioso.	It's boring.
Ha ragione.	You are right.

Activity A

Che pensa? (What do you think?) Write *è noioso* or *è divertente* to indicate what you think about each activity.

1

_____

2

_____

3

_____

4

_____

Activity B

What do you say if you want to…

1   …ask someone what he or she is doing?

_____

2   …ask someone what he or she usually does?

_____

3   …tell what you usually do *durante l'inverno*?

_____

4   …tell someone he or she is right?

_____

Your Turn

Complete the phrases with your favorite or not so favorite activities.

1   _____ è divertente.

2   _____ è noioso.

3   _____ è divertente.

4   _____ è noioso.

SMART PRONUNCIATION

The consonants *c* and *g* can be either soft or hard according to the letters that follow. They are hard in front of *a, o, u*. Examples: *casa* [kah-sah], *gatto* [gaht-toh]. They are soft in front of *e* and *i*. Examples: *gelato* [jeh-lah-toh], *ciao* [chah-oh]. *Ch* and *gh* are used in front of *e* and *i* to make the sound hard: *chiesa* [kyeh-zah], *ghiaccio* [ghyah-chyoh].

LESSON 7

Words to Know

Core Words

I vestiti (Clothes)

il cappotto	coat
il costume	bathing suit
la giacca	jacket
i guanti	gloves
la maglietta	T-shirt
i pantaloncini	shorts
la sciarpa	scarf

Le stagioni (Seasons)

la primavera	spring
l'estate	summer
l'autunno	autumn
l'inverno	winter

Extra Words

correre	to run
giocare	to play
nuotare	to swim
portare/indossare	to wear
viaggiare	to travel
le scarpe	shoes

Activity A

Write the Italian word for each image.

1 _____

2 _____

3 _____

Activity B

Use the words in the box to name the season in each picture.

> l'inverno   la primavera   l'estate   l'autunno

1 _____

2 _____

3 _____

4 _____

Activity C

Write the Italian word or words to complete each sentence.

1 Porto la _____ in autunno.
               jacket

2 Tu porti i _____ in inverno.
               gloves

3 Lei porta una_____ in primavera.
               T-shirt

4 Mio zio porta i _____ in estate.
               shorts

LESSON 8
Smart Grammar

The Present Progressive

The present progressive tense indicates an action that is currently taking place.

Verbs that end in –are

stare (conjugated) + verb stem + *–ando*
Example *giocare* ⟶ *giocando*
Lei sta giocando.   She is playing.

Verbs that end in –ere and –ire

stare (conjugated) + verb stem + *––endo*
Example *correre* ⟶ *correndo*
Stiamo correndo.   We are running.
Example *partire* (to leave) ⟶ *partendo*
Loro stanno partendo.   They are leaving.

The verb *stare* (to stay)

The irregular verb *stare* is used to form the progressive tense.

io	sto	I stay
tu	stai	you stay
Lei	sta	you stay
lui/lei	sta	he/she stays
noi	stiamo	we stay
voi	state	you stay
loro	stanno	they stay

Activity A

Write the present progressive form of *viaggiare*.

io   _____
tu   _____
Lei   _____
lui/lei _____
noi   _____
voi   _____
loro   _____

Activity B

Look at each picture and write what is happening.

1   io: viaggiare

_____

2   lui: giocare

_____

3   loro: correre

_____

4   tu: nuotare

_____

The verb *giocare* (to play)

The verb *giocare* (like all verbs ending in *-gare*) adds an *-h* to the second person singular *tu* and the first person plural *noi* in order to maintain the hard sound of the consonant c. Example: *tu giochi, noi giochiamo*. It also requires the preposition *a* before the things that you play. Example: *Gioco a calcio* (I play soccer).

Activity C

Write sentences in Italian saying who plays *a calcio*.

1   (Maria) _____
2   (noi)   _____
3   (io)   _____
4   (tu)   _____

Activity D

A cosa gioca? (What do you play?) Use the correct form of "to play" to answer the question.

1   _____
pallavolo

2   _____
golf

3   _____
carte

4   _____
calcio

Review

Activity A

How would you translate the following sentences?

1 I am studying. _____

2 He is running. _____

3 We are leaving. _____

4 It is raining. _____

5 She is swimming. _____

Activity B

Write the Italian adjective in the correct place.

1 la _____ macchina _____ (blu)

2 una _____ casa _____ (bella)

3 un _____ ragazzo _____ (giovane)

4 un _____ uomo _____ (italiano)

5 un _____ cappotto _____ (caro)

Activity C

Complete the word search to find words related to the weather and seasons.

> vento   sole   caldo   freddo   estate
> piovere   primavera   neve   temperatura

```
B  P  E  V  Z  L  Z  S  C  S  H  N  W  Y  J
X  C  L  A  C  H  A  Q  U  E  T  E  W  V  V
Q  P  Y  C  X  Q  Z  M  K  D  Y  V  P  Y  C
E  D  S  L  A  P  R  I  M  A  V  E  R  A  E
R  D  O  B  M  N  A  B  R  Z  E  K  P  E  S
E  A  L  F  L  M  S  V  L  E  A  D  O  I  T
V  Q  E  A  T  E  M  P  E  R  A  T  U  R  A
O  Z  Z  Z  Q  G  A  L  Q  N  W  P  E  H  T
I  E  S  T  A  C  A  L  I  D  T  D  L  L  E
P  I  J  U  G  A  R  C  A  L  D  O  J  K  W
B  K  V  F  Z  R  H  V  R  E  P  J  U  O  D
S  Q  W  R  J  P  K  A  P  P  P  J  R  N  Y  U
I  T  O  D  D  E  R  F  D  B  X  L  Q  X  N
```

Activity D

Che tempo fa? (What's the weather like?) Maria is going out, but before leaving, she checks the weather report. Write in Italian what each image tells her about today's weather.

 1

_____

 2

_____

 3

_____

Challenge

You've studied the present progressive and its relationship to weather. Looking back at the phrases and grammar lessons, how would you say that you play soccer when it's raining?

Internet Activity

Wonder what the weather is like in Italy? Go to **www. berlitzbooks.com/5minute** for a site on the Italian forecast. Choose four cities and look at the temperature. Then say in Italian whether the weather is nice or bad.

In this unit you will:
- use vocabulary related to shopping and payment.
- ask for pieces of clothing and sizes.
- make comparisons with "more than" and "less than."
- learn reflexive verbs such as *provarsi* (to try on) and *vestirsi* (to get dressed).
- use indefinite pronouns such as *qualcuno* (someone) and *qualcosa* (something).

LESSON 1

Il negozio d'abbiglia-mento

Dialogue

Anna is at *un negozio d'abbigliamento* (a clothing store). She is looking for a dress. Listen as she talks to *il commesso* (the shop assistant).

Commesso Buon giorno. Posso aiutarla?

Anna Sto cercando un vestito.

Commesso I vestiti sono qui. Che taglia porta?

Anna La M, grazie.

Commesso Bene. Vuole provare il vestito blu?

Anna Sì, grazie.

Commesso Come le sta?

Anna Mi va stretto. Posso provare la L?

Commesso Sì, va bene.

Activity A

Circle the correct picture.

1 Which item is Anna looking for?

  a   b   c

2 What size does Anna want?

a  *small*   b  *medium*   c *large*

3 What color does Anna want?

a   b   c

Activity B

Match the Italian questions with their English translations.

1 Posso aiutarla?

  a How can I help you?
  b How would you like to pay?

2 Che taglia porta?

  a What color would you like?
  b What size do you need?

3 Come le sta?

  a How does it fit?
  b What size dress do you want?

LESSON 2

Smart Phrases

Core Phrases

Che taglia porta?	What size do you need?
Porto la (taglia) _____.	I need a (size) _____.
Come le sta?	How does it fit?
Mi va stretto/largo.	It is tight/loose.
Le serve altro?	Do you need anything else?
Posso aiutarla?	Can I help you?
Sto cercando _____.	I'm looking for ____.
Vorrei comprare un/una _____.	I want to buy a _____.
Vuole provarsi ____?	Do you want to try ___ on?

Activity A

Choose the best response.

1 Buon giorno. Posso aiutarla?

a Sto cercando una gonna.

b La gonna è piccola.

2 Che taglia porta?

a Porto una taglia grande.

b Vorrei comprare un maglione.

3 Vuole provarsi il vestito?

a Sto cercando una camicia.

b Sì, grazie.

4 Le serve altro?

a No, grazie.

b Mi sta stretto.

Activity B

Respond with one of the phrases you've learned.

1 Posso aiutarla?

_____.
Say that you are looking for a dress.

2 Le serve altro?

_____.
Say that you need a medium shirt.

3 Le serve altro?

_____.
Say that you want to buy a skirt.

4 Che taglia porta?

_____.
Say that you wear a small.

SMART TIP

The word *altro* is very versatile. *Altro* is the Italian equivalent of both "anything" and "something." So, if someone asks you *Altro?* (Anything else?) you can respond *Sì, vorrei qualcos'altro.* (Yes, I'd like something else).

Words to Know

Core Words

L'abbigliamento (Clothing)

i calzini	socks
la camicia	shirt
la cravatta	tie
la gonna	skirt
il maglione	sweater
i pantaloni	pants
il vestito	dress/suit
i vestiti	clothes

Le taglie (Sizes)

la XS	extra small
la S	small
la M	medium
la L	large
la XL	extra large

I colori (Colors)

arancione	orange
bianco	white
blu	blue
giallo	yellow
marrone	brown
nero	black
rosa	pink
rosso	red
verde	green
viola	purple

SMART TIP

With the exceptions of *blu*, *rosa* and *viola*, which don't change form, be sure to use the correct form of adjectives of color, based on gender and quantity. So, for example, white is *bianco* (m)/*bianca* (f)/*bianchi* (m, pl.)/*bianche* (f, pl.).

Activity A

Label the clothing in Italian.

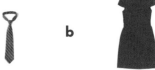

1 _____
2 _____
3 _____
4 _____
5 _____

Activity B

Read each sentence, then circle the item you are looking for.

1 Sto cercando una camicia rosa.

     a   b

2 Sto cercando una cravatta rossa.

     a   b

3 Sto cercando una camicia L.

     a   b

4 Sto cercando un vestito nero.

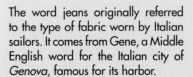

     a   b

CULTURE TIP

The word jeans originally referred to the type of fabric worn by Italian sailors. It comes from Gene, a Middle English word for the Italian city of *Genova*, famous for its harbor.

LESSON 4

Smart Grammar

Reflexive Verbs

- *Vestirsi* (to get dressed, literally: to dress oneself) and *provarsi* (to try on) are reflexive verbs. Reflexive verbs are for actions a person does to, at or for himself or herself.

- To conjugate a reflexive verb, drop the *-arsi*, *-ersi* and *-irsi* endings, and follow the regular conjugation pattern of *-are*, *-ere* and *-ire* verbs using a reflexive pronoun before the verb (see below).

Reflexive Pronouns

io	mi	myself
tu	ti	yourself
Lei	si	yourself
lui/lei	si	himself/herself
noi	ci	ourselves
voi	vi	yourselves
loro	si	themselves

Vestirsi (to get dressed)

io	mi vesto	I get dressed
tu	ti vesti	you get dressed
Lei	si veste	you get dressed
lui/lei	si veste	he/she gets dressed
noi	ci vestiamo	we get dressed
voi	vi vestite	you get dressed
loro	si vestono	they get dressed

Activity A

Fill in the blanks with the correct reflexive pronoun.

1 Lui _____ veste alle otto.

2 Noi _____ proviamo i pantaloni.

3 Loro _____ vestono di mattina.

4 Tu _____ provi una camicia.

Activity B

Write the correct conjugation of the verb *vestirsi* to complete each sentence.

1 Loro si _____ alle sette.

2 Ti _____ alle nove.

3 Mi _____ per la festa.

4 Il bambino si _____ da solo.

5 Ci _____ di mattina.

SMART TIP

When a sentence includes *potere* (to be able, can), *dovere* (to have to, must) or *volere* (to want), you can place the reflexive pronoun before these verbs (e.g., *Mi voglio vestire*, I want to get dressed) or after the main verb without the final e (e.g., *Voglio vestirmi*).

Your Turn

Here are some other common reflexive verbs: *alzarsi* (to get up), *lavarsi* (to wash), *svegliarsi* (to wake up), *mettersi* (to put on). Choose one of them and complete the conjugation, paying attention to the ending. If you're not sure, look at the answer key in the back of the book.

io	mi	
tu	ti	
Lei	si	
lui/lei	si	
noi	ci	
voi	vi	
loro	si	

Come vuole pagare?

How Will You Pay?

Carefully read the shopping advertisement. Look at the words in the vocabulary box to help you.

Moda Italia

Venite al negozio Moda Italia per una vendita promozionale!
I vestiti di D&G e Armani hanno il 50% di sconto. Un affare!
Le camicie di Versace e altri abiti firmati hanno invece il 30% di sconto.

Now look at the ad for *Stile italiano*. Note the differences between this ad and the previous one.

STILE ITALIANO

Venite al negozio Stile italiano per una vendita promozionale!
I vestiti di D&G e Armani hanno il 20% di sconto. Un affare!
Le camicie di Versace e altri abiti firmati hanno invece il 40% di sconto.

Quanto costano le gonne?

Costano €40. Non accettiamo carte di credito.

Accettate carte di credito?

Sì le accettiamo.

abiti firmati	designer clothes
50% di sconto	50% off
un affare	a bargain
vendita promozionale/saldi	sales
Venite!	Come!

Activity A

Circle the correct answer. Use the ad to help you.

1 Who is the dress designer?
   a D&G   b Versace

2 Which has the larger discount?
   a dresses   b shirts

3 Are the shirts on sale?
   a yes   b no

4 Does Moda Italia take credit and debit cards?
   a yes   b no

Activity B

Compare the ads and circle the correct answer.

1 Which discount is greater?
   a shirts at Moda Italia   b shirts at Stile italiano

2 Are dresses at Moda Italia cheaper or more expensive than the dresses at Stile italiano?
   a more expensive   b cheaper

3 Are D&G and Armani on sale at both shops?
   a yes   b no

4 Does Stile italiano take credit cards?
   a yes   b no

CULTURE TIP

Italy is part of the European Union and its currency is the *euro* (€). The *euro* replaced Italy's *lira*. In Switzerland, the Swiss franc—*franco svizzero* in Italian— is still used. However, the euro is accepted near the Swiss borders and in regions with many tourists. Note that, since *euro* is a word of foreign origin, it doesn't change form in the plural: *un euro, due euro.*

LESSON 6

Smart Phrases

Core Phrases

Accettate carte di credito e bancomat/assegni?	Do you accept credit and debit cards/checks?
Sì, accettiamo_____.	Yes, we accept____.
Quanto costa la gonna?	How much is the skirt?
Quanto costano i pantaloni?	How much are the pants?
Costa/Costano poco!	It's/They're cheap!
(Non) è (molto) caro!	That's (not/very) expensive!
Vorrei pagare con la carta di credito.	I would like to pay by credit card.

Extra Phrases

Ecco il resto/lo scontrino.	Here's your change/receipt.
Vorrei comprarlo/comprarla.	I would like to buy it. (m/f)
Vorrei comprarli/comprarle.	I would like to buy them. (m/f)
Do solo un'occhiata.	I'm just looking.

Activity A

What do you say when you want to…

1   …ask if the shop accepts debit cards?

   _____

2   …ask how much a skirt is?

   _____

3   …ask if the shop accepts checks?

   _____

4   …say you would like to pay by credit card?

   _____

5   …ask how much pants are?

   _____

Activity B

Look at each picture and choose the word that best completes each statement.

> care   poco   molto   cara

1

   Sono _____.

2

   È _____.

3

   Costa _____.

4

   Costano _____.

CULTURE TIP

Italians like to be always at their best. The expression *fare bella figura* literally means to make a good impression and refers to a philosophy of life. Notice that Italians often dress well, even for informal occasions.

LESSON 7

Words to Know

Core Words

l'assegno	check
il bancomat	debit card
la carta di credito	credit card
i contanti	cash
lo scontrino	receipt
i soldi	money

Extra Words

il cambio	exchange rate
i centesimi	cents
il portafoglio	wallet
il resto	change
gli spiccioli	small change

Activity A

Complete the sentences with the appropriate Italian word.

1 Accettate un _____?
    check

3 Ecco _____.
    the receipt

Activity B

Fill in the blanks with the correct Italian words to complete Marco's thought bubble. Use the English translations as clues.

Ho 500 _____ in _____
        euros   cash
nel mio portafoglio. Ho anche una

_____. Voglio comprare molti
credit card

vestiti perché _____ è favorevole.
              exchange rate

SMART TIPS

- If you want to say you'll pay with something, use the Italian preposition *con*.
  Vorrei pagare con la carta di credito.   I'd like to pay with a credit card.

- There is an exception for cash. You would use the preposition *in*: *Vorrei pagare in contanti.*

2 Vorrei pagare con _____.
                    the debit card

4 Non ho _____.
          money

LESSON 8

Smart Grammar

Più di (More Than) and *meno di* (Less Than)

The expressions *più di* and *meno di* are used to make comparisons. Notice that you need a definite article after nouns. *Di* + the definite article becomes one word: *di + il = del, di + lo = dello, di + l' = dell', di + la = della, di + i = dei, di + gli = degli, di + le = delle*. The phrases are used in the same way as their English equivalents, for example:

Marco ha più soldi di Paola.	Marco has more money than Paola.
Paola ha meno soldi di Marco.	Paola has less money than Marco.
La camicia costa più della cravatta.	The shirt costs more than the tie.
La cravatta costa meno della camicia.	The tie costs less than the shirt.

Activity A

Look at the items on the rack, then decide which ones cost more and which ones cost less. Write *più di* or *meno di* in the blanks to complete the phrases.

1 Il vestito costa _____ camicia.

2 I pantaloni costano _____ maglione.

3 La camicia costa _____vestito.

4 Il maglione costa _____ pantaloni.

€60

€45

€40

€100

Indefinite Pronouns

Indefinite pronouns are used when talking about an unspecified noun. There are many other indefinite pronouns in Italian. Here are a few:

qualcuno/qualcuna (m/f)
someone, somebody, anyone or anybody

Example Conosco qualcuno che vive in Canada.
I know someone who lives in Canada.

qualcosa
something (when followed by an adjective, add *di* before the adjective that is always masculine)
Example Cerco qualcosa di speciale.
I am looking for something special.

nessuno/nessuna (m/f)
no one, nobody, none

Example Nessuno di loro mangia carne.
None of them eats meat.

niente, nulla
nothing, anything (when followed by an adjective you need *di* before the adjective that is always masculine

Example In quel negozio non c'è niente di bello.
In that shop there is nothing nice.

Activity B

Circle the correct indefinite pronoun for each sentence.

1 **Qualcuno**   **Qualcosa**   vuole mangiare?

2 **Niente**   **Nessuno**   di loro studia italiano.

3 Di sera leggo   **qualcuno**   **qualcosa**.

> **SMART TIP**
>
> Use the word *come* (equal, same) when comparing items with the same price.
>
> *La camicia costa come i pantaloni.* (The shirt costs the same as the pants).

Unit 7 Review

Activity A

As you've learned, reflexive verbs are used when applying action to oneself. Look at the sentences and include the reflexive pronoun.

1 _____ provo la camicia.

2 Giulia _____ veste con abiti firmati.

3 _____ vestiamo dello stesso colore.

4 _____ provi i pantaloni.

Challenge

Divertirsi (to have fun) is an important irregular reflexive verb. Try to complete the conjugation chart. One is done for you.

io	mi	
tu	ti	diverti
Lei	si	
lui/lei	si	
noi	ci	
voi	vi	
loro	si	

Activity B

Conjugate the verb *costare* (for help, refer to Lesson 6) and tell which items are more and less expensive. Write two sentences for each pair, one using *più di* and another with *meno di*.

Activity C

Based on the images, complete the crossword puzzle using the correct Italian term. Remember to include the definite article for all nouns.

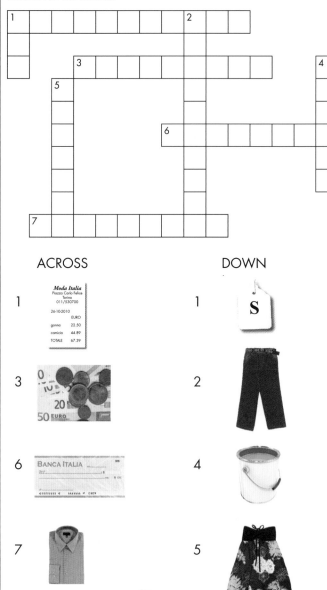

ACROSS

1 Moda Italia — Piazza Carlo Felice, Torino, 011/530700 — 26-10-2010 — EURO — gonna 22.50 — camicia 44.89 — TOTALE 67.39

3

6 BANCA ITALIA

7

DOWN

1 S

2

4

5

Internet Activity

Go to **www.berlitzbooks.com/5minute** for a list of Italian-language online shops to browse. Navigate each site and look at what is featured. Make sure you click on the Italian version. Some sites may have different pages for *Uomo* or *Donna*. What is your favorite *camicia*? What are your favorite *pantaloni*?

In this unit you will:
- ask for directions.
- talk about location.
- discuss an itinerary.
- use the irregular verb *andare* (to go).

LESSON 1

Dov'è la stazione?

Dialogue

A couple from Milan is visiting Rome for the first time. They are looking for directions so they can get to the *Colosseo*. Listen as Giovanni and Barbara discuss where to go.

Barbara Noi siamo qui, alla Stazione Termini. Come facciamo ad arrivare al Colosseo?

Giovanni Guarda la cartina. Il Colosseo è vicino a Via Cavour. Possiamo prendere l'autobus o la metropolitana.

Barbara Non è lontano. Andiamo a piedi!

Giovanni La fermata della metropolitana è davanti alla stazione.

Barbara No, è meglio camminare, così sappiamo dove sono le vie e le chiese. Voglio vedere i monumenti più importanti.

Giovanni Va bene. Andiamo!

SMART TIPS

- *Andiamo!* is a very common term in Italian. It means "Let's go!"
- To encourage someone to do something use the *noi* form of a verb. For example: *Chiediamo dove andare* (Let's ask where to go), or *Prendiamo una guida* (Let's get a guide).

Activity A

Look at the clues. Try to guess the meaning of the following verbs. Write the English verb on the line.

arrivare _____

prendere _____

camminare _____

Activity B

Answer the following questions in Italian. If you don't know a word, try to figure out the meaning through the context of the dialogue, then look at the Words to Know page to check your vocabulary.

1 Where are Giovanni and Barbara? _____

2 Where do they want to go? _____

3 How can they get there? _____

4 Why does Barbara want to walk? _____

LESSON 2
Words to Know

Core Words

I luoghi (Places)

la banca	bank
la biblioteca	library
la chiesa	church
la fermata dell'autobus	bus stop
la stazione della metropolitana	subway station
il monumento	monument
la posta/l'ufficio postale	post office
la scuola	school
la stazione (ferroviaria)	train station
il supermercato	supermarket

La posizione (Location)

a destra	to the right
a sinistra	to the left
all'angolo	on the corner
davanti (a)	in front (of)
dietro	behind
lontano (da)	far (from)
tra/fra	between
vicino (a)	near (to)

Extra Words

l'isolato	block
la piazza	square

SMART TIPS

- Note that with *vicino a, davanti a, lontano da* the prepositions *a* and *da* combine with the article in front of the noun. Examples: *vicino alla chiesa* (near the church), *lontano dall'ufficio postale* (far from the post office).

- To indicate that something is to the left or right of something else, use the preposition *a*. *La biblioteca è a sinistra della scuola.* (The library is to the left of the school).

Activity A
Label each building, station or stop with the correct Italian word.

library

subway station

school

church

train station

bus stop

post office

supermarket

SMART TIP

The word for post office is *ufficio postale*. However, it is very common to use the word *posta*, which also means mail: *Vado alla posta* (I go to the post office). *Ho ricevuto molta posta* (I received a lot of mail).

Activity B
Circle the appropriate term to describe where each thing is located.

1 La stazione della metropolitana è _____ della biblioteca.

    a a destra   **b a sinistra**

2 La scuola è _____ stazione (ferroviaria).

    a lontano dalla   **b vicino alla**

3 Il supermercato è _____ biblioteca.

    a lontano dalla   **b vicino alla**

4 La fermata della metropolitana è _____ la biblioteca e la scuola.

    a dietro   **b fra**

LESSON 3

Smart Phrases

Core Phrases

Come faccio ad arrivare a _____?	How do I get to _____?
Dov'è _____?	Where is _____?
Per andare a _____, prenda l'autobus numero _____.	To get to _____, take bus number _____.
Prendiamo una cartina!	Let's get a map!
Voglio prendere il treno/ l'autobus/la metropolitana.	I want to take the train/ bus/subway.
La stazione (ferroviaria) è vicino alla scuola.	The train station is near the school.

Extra Phrases

Grazie/Molte grazie/ Grazie mille.	Thank you/Thanks a lot/ Thanks a million.
Prego.	You're welcome.
Scusi.	Excuse me.

Activity A

Look at each picture. Write in Italian that you want to use that mode of transportation. Then ask where you can find the station or the stop.

1
_____
_____

2
_____
_____

3
_____
_____

Activity B

What do you say if you want to…

1   …ask where the train station is?

_____
_____

2   …ask how to get to the subway stop?

_____
_____

3   …tell someone the train station is near the school?

_____
_____

4   …say "let's get a map"?

_____
_____

Activity C

You are helping a tourist with directions. He needs to go to the *piazza*. To get there, he has to go to the bus stop and take bus number 9. Then, to go to the church, he has to take the train. Read his questions and tell him what to do.

1   Come faccio ad arrivare a Piazza Garibaldi?

_____
_____
_____

2   Come faccio ad arrivare alla chiesa?

_____
_____
_____

Your Turn

You want to go to the bus station. Ask—out loud—where it is and how to get there. Don't forget to be polite!

LESSON 4
Smart Grammar

SMART TIP

These are some cases where you do not use an article with the prepositions *a* or *in*:

Andare a casa/a scuola/a teatro (to go home/to school/to the theater).

Andare in chiesa/in biblioteca/in banca (to go to church/to the library/to the bank).

The verb *andare* (to go)

The verb *andare* is irregular. The chart shows its conjugation in the present tense.

io	vado	I go
tu	vai	you go
Lei	va	you go
lui/lei	va	he/she goes
noi	andiamo	we go
voi	andate	you go
loro	vanno	they go

Examples

Vado in chiesa.   I go to church.

Andiamo al supermercato.   We go to the supermarket.

Activity A

Fill in the blanks with the correct form of *andare*.

1   Loro _____ in biblioteca.

2   Lei _____ alla fermata dell'autobus.

3   Noi _____ all'ufficio postale.

4   Tu _____ alla stazione.

Activity B

After the verb *andare,* in most cases you need the preposition *a*, which combines with the article in front of the noun. Example: *Luca va all'ufficio postale* (Luca goes to the post office). Can you put the right contraction in front of the following nouns?

1   Luisa va _____ ristorante.

2   Noi andiamo _____ stazione.

3   Loro vanno _____ ufficio postale.

4   Marco va _____ supermercato.

5   I bambini vanno _____ zoo.

Activity C

Write sentences with the verb *andare* to tell where you think someone will go. Remember to use the right contractions when needed.

1 _____

_____

2 _____

_____

3 _____

_____

4 _____

_____

CULTURE TIP

If you are traveling from city to city in Italy, airfare can be expensive. A good alternative between big cities is the train system. It's reliable, fast and easy, and you may even make a friend along the way. If you want to travel at high speed and get from Milan to Rome in just 3 hours and 30 minutes, look for *Frecciarossa* trains, the new generation, fastest trains.

Arrivi e partenze

Arrivals and Departures

Read the e-mail from Dario to Enrico with information about their trip to Pisa. Then answer the questions below.

```
⊖ ○ ○

Data:     martedì 26 agosto
Da:       Dario
A:        Enrico
Oggetto:  Pisa


Ciao Enrico,
finalmente andiamo in vacanza!
Andiamo a Pisa! Conosci Pisa? Io non
la conosco. Ho i biglietti dell'aereo
e la prenotazione dell'albergo. La
mia valigia è già pronta.
Queste sono le informazioni: Il
numero del volo è 611. Partiamo da
New York alle 17:00 e arriviamo a
Roma il giorno dopo alle 7:20. Poi
partiamo alle 9:40 e arriviamo a Pisa
alle 10:45. Dall'aeroporto prendiamo
l'autobus fino all'albergo. Ci vediamo
all'aeroporto.
A presto,
Dario
```

SMART TIPS

- The prepositions *da* is equivalent to the word "from" in English. When it is followed by an article, a contraction is formed. For example: *Partiamo dall'aeroporto di New York* (We leave from the airport in New York).

- *Fino* means "until" or "as far as." *Prendo l'autobus fino all'albergo* (I take the bus as far as the hotel).

- You use *già*, which always follows the verb, to mean "already." *Ho già la valigia pronta* (I already have the suitcase ready).

Activity A

Circle the correct answer for each question.

1 Where are Dario and Enrico going?
   a New York   **b Pisa**

2 Do they have a hotel reservation?
   a no   **b yes**

3 What time does the plane leave New York?
   a 5 AM   **b 5 PM**

4 How are they getting to the hotel from the airport?
   a by bus   **b by car**

Activity B

Dario and Enrico's flight itinerary has changed. Look at the new information and complete Dario's e-mail.

Alitalia			AZ611
Departs	**Time**	**Arrives**	**Time**
New York JFK International Airport	5:30 PM	Rome, Fiumicino Airport	8:00 AM
Rome, Fiumicino Airport	9:40 AM	Pisa, Galileo Galilei Airport	10:45 AM

```
⊖ ○ ○

Data:     mercoledì 27 agosto
Da:       Dario
A:        Enrico
Oggetto:  Pisa


Ciao Enrico,
ho nuove informazioni sul volo del
pomeriggio. L'aereo parte da New York
alle _____. Arriviamo a Roma
alle_____.
```

LESSON 6

Words to Know

Core Words

l'aereo	plane
l'aeroporto	airport
i bagagli	luggage
il biglietto	ticket
il passaporto	passport
la vacanza	vacation
la valigia	suitcase
il viaggio	trip
il volo	flight
il volo diretto	nonstop flight

Extra Words

l'albergo	hotel
la dogana	customs
la prenotazione	reservation
lo scalo	stopover

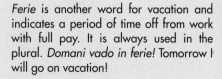

CULTURE TIP

If you plan to visit Italy for fewer than 90 days, you need just a valid passport. But if you plan to stay longer, you need to apply for a *visto* (visa).

SMART TIP

Ferie is another word for vacation and indicates a period of time off from work with full pay. It is always used in the plural. *Domani vado in ferie!* Tomorrow I will go on vacation!

Activity A

Draw a line to match each picture with the correct Italian word.

1 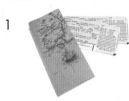   **a** il passaporto

2    **b** il biglietto

3    **c** l'aereo

4    **d** la valigia

5   **e** l'aeroporto

Activity B

Pick the correct Italian term from the choices below.

1 luggage
  a i bagagli   **b** il passaporto   **c** valigia
2 flight
  a il volo   **b** dogana   **c** l'aereo
3 trip
  a la vacanza   **b** il viaggio   **c** il biglietto
4 vacation
  a il viaggio   **b** la vacanza   **c** il volo

LESSON 7

Smart Phrases

C21, C22, C23
C24, C25, C26 Gates
C4
C6

Core Phrases

Quando parte il prossimo volo per Pisa?	When is the next flight to Pisa?
Il volo parte a/all'/alle ____.	The flight leaves at ____.
Il volo arriva a/all'/alle ____.	The flight arrives at ____.
È un volo diretto o bisogna fare scalo?	Is it a direct flight or is there a stopover?
Qual è l'uscita?	Which is the departing/ arriving gate?
Quanto costa il biglietto?	How much does the ticket cost?
Il volo costa 500 euro andata e ritorno.	The flight costs 500 euros round-trip.

Extra Phrases

A presto!	Till soon!
Ci vediamo all'aeroporto/ in albergo!	See you at the airport/ hotel!
Finalmente!	At last!

Activity A

What do you say if you want to…

1   …tell your friend that your flight leaves at 12:30?

_____

2   …ask which is the departing gate?

_____

3   …ask how much the ticket is?

_____

4   …tell your friend that you will see him/her at the hotel?

_____

Activity B

Armando is looking for the next available flight to Rome. He goes up to a ticket agent and asks him a few questions. Circle the best responses to Armando's questions.

1   Quando parte il prossimo volo per Roma?
   a Il volo parte alle otto.
   b Il volo arriva alle dieci.

2   È un volo diretto o bisogna fare scalo?
   a Il volo è diretto.
   b Il volo arriva domani.

3   Quanto costa il biglietto?
   a Il volo arriva alle quattordici.
   b Il biglietto costa 500 euro.

Activity C

Look at the chart and answer the questions below.

PARTENZE		
Ora	Destinazione	Volo
16:15	Roma	AZ5258
16:35	Milano	AZ5259
17:00	Catania	AZ448058
17:00	Venezia	AZ7250
17:20	Pisa	AZ7251
17:25	Napoli	AZ4432

1   A che ora parte il prossimo volo per Roma?

_____

2   Che volo parte alle 17:00?

_____

Your Turn

You work for Alitalia and you have to announce the next flight to Milan: Flight 1699, departs at 10:23 AM, arrives at 1:30 PM. Use your new phrases and vocabulary to give information about the flight.

SMART TIP

If you want to buy a round-trip ticket you'll ask for *un biglietto andata e ritorno. Sola andata* is a one-way ticket.

LESSON 8

Smart Grammar

The verbs *conoscere* and *sapere* (to know)

Conoscere means to know people and places—not facts, skills or ideas. *Sapere*, an irregular verb, is to know facts and ideas. The chart shows its irregular conjugation in the present tense.

io	so	I know
tu	sai	you know
Lei	sa	you know
lui/lei	sa	he/she knows
noi	sappiamo	we know
voi	sapete	you know
loro	sanno	they know

Examples

Conosco Laura.	I know Laura.
Loro conoscono l'Italia.	They know Italy.
Io so parlare italiano.	I can speak Italian.
Loro sanno che ora è.	They know what time it is.

SMART TIP

Use the expression *Lo so!* for "Yes, I know!" Example: *Sai che parto domani per Roma? Lo so.* (Do you know that I leave tomorrow for Rome? Yes, I know.)

Activity A

Choose *conoscere* or *sapere* for each sentence.

1 Carlo _____ giocare a calcio.

2 Noi _____ la Svizzera.

3 Loro _____ dov'è il ristorante.

4 Io non _____ l'Italia.

5 Tu _____ parlare tre lingue.

6 Maria _____ bene Piero.

Direct Object Pronouns

mi	me
ti	you
La	you
lo	him/it
la	her/it
ci	us
vi	you
li	them (m)
le	them (f)

Examples

Luigi mi conosce.	Luigi knows me.
Io lo studio.	I study it.
Ti conosco.	I know you.

Activity B

Change the sentences so they use direct object pronouns. Note that direct object pronouns always precede the verb.

1 Io mangio la pasta. _____

2 Lei studia italiano. _____

3 Tu conosci le persone. _____

4 Loro prendono i biglietti. _____

Your Turn

Do you know them? Look at each picture and write a sentence using *conoscere* to indicate if you know or don't know each person, place or animal. Remember to use direct object pronouns.

1  2

_____ _____

3  4

_____ _____

Activity A

Read Mario's postcard from his trip to Venice. He didn't conjugate the verbs *andare* and *sapere* correctly. Cross out the mistakes and rewrite the verbs using the correct form.

Cara Carla,
Sono a Venezia con mia madre.
Domani vai a Verona. So dov'è
Verona? Verona è molto bella. Mia
madre la conosce bene. Poi andate a
Roma sabato.
Un abbraccio,
Mario

Activity B

Fill in the blanks to complete Sara's plan for her trip to Milan.

Il mio viaggio a Milano

_____ a Milano. _____ otto di
   I go   My flight leaves at
mattina. Arrivo _____ alle sei.
                      at the airport
È molto presto! Ho già il _____,
                      ticket
_____ e _____. Arrivo a Milano alle
  luggage   passport
ventidue e cerco _____ per andare in albergo.
               a train station
L'albergo è _____ teatro alla Scala.
        near the
Io lo conosco. È anche _____.
               behind a church
Domani, _____ per andare
      I want to take the subway
a vedere il Duomo. Ho bisogno di un biglietto della

metropolitana.

Activity C

Alfonso and Stefania are visiting Italy. They are looking for the post office. Write the correct Italian word or phrase to complete their dialogue.

Alfonso _____ l'ufficio postale?
           Where is

Stefania _____ una cartina!
           Let's get

Alfonso Guarda la cartina. L'ufficio postale è
_____.
     to the right of the library

Stefania Sì, è anche _____.
             behind the supermarket

Alfonso Questa è _____.
            the bus stop

Stefania Ecco l'autobus. _____ prendiamo?
                     It

Challenge

As you know, *sapere* is irregular and means "to know" with facts, ideas and how to do things. Do you remember its conjugation? Can you complete the chart?

io	_____
tu	_____
Lei	_____
lui/lei	_____
noi	_____
voi	_____
loro	_____

Internet Activity

Go to **www.berlitzbooks.com/5minute** and look for the site of the Italian Railway system. Imagine you are in Milan and you want to go to Rome. Choose whether you want to go *andata* (one way) or *andata e ritorno* (round trip). Write *Milano* under *Da dove vuoi partire?* (Where do you want to leave from?) and write *Roma* under *Dove vuoi arrivare?* (Where do you want to arrive?). Choose the dates and the time: *giorno, mese, anno, ora* and then click on *invia* (go). You will be able to see the schedule and see the *importo* (amount) you need to pay.

In this unit you will:
- **describe different professions and compare different jobs.**
- **read a job application in Italian.**
- **conjugate regular verbs in the past with the auxiliary *avere* and learn some common irregular past participles.**
- **learn expressions of time using *da* and *per*.**

LESSON 1

Un colloquio di lavoro

SMART TIP

The preposition *di* (about) can be used with the verb *parlare* to talk about the topic or theme of a book, movie or article. Example: *L'articolo parla di economia.* (The article is about the economy.) When the noun is followed by an adjective, use a definite article, which combines with *di*: *L'articolo parla dell'economia italiana* (The article is about the Italian economy).

The preposition *su* + the article are used to indicate a topic you read or wrote on: *Ho letto un libro sull'Italia* (I read a book on Italy).

Dialogue

Claudia is on a job interview for *La Repubblica*, a famous newspaper. Listen as her potential employer asks about her previous job and responsibilities.

Datore di lavoro Dove ha lavorato?

Claudia Ho lavorato per il giornale *La Stampa*.

Datore di lavoro Ha scritto articoli per questo giornale?

Claudia Ho scritto vari articoli.

Datore di lavoro Su quali argomenti?

Claudia Sulla cultura italiana. Questi sono gli articoli.

Datore di lavoro Questi articoli sono molto buoni! È assunta.

Claudia Grazie mille! Quando inizio?

Datore di lavoro Lunedì prossimo. Ci vediamo lunedì alle otto e mezzo.

SMART PRONUNCIATION

Remember that in Italian *h* is always silent. The *h* used in the conjugation of *avere* (*ho, hai,* etc.) is not pronounced. Also, English words that begin with an *h*, used in the Italian language—such as *hotel* or *hamburger*—are pronounced without aspirating the *h*.

Activity A

Circle the correct answer for each question.

1 Where did Claudia work before?

    a rivista   **b giornale**

2 What did Claudia do at her previous job?

    a ha insegnato   **b ha scritto**

3 What does Claudia show the employer?

    a articoli   **b foto**

4 Does Claudia get the job?

    a sì   **b no**

Activity B

Choose a word from the box to complete each sentence.

> ha scritto   cultura   inizia   ha lavorato

1 Claudia _____ per un giornale.

2 Claudia _____ articoli per un giornale.

3 Ha scritto articoli sulla _____.

4 Claudia _____ lunedì alle otto e mezzo.

LESSON 2

Words to Know

Core Words

la classe	classroom
il giornale	newspaper
il giornalista/la giornalista	journalist (m/f)
la lezione	class
la professione	profession
il professore/la professoressa	teacher or professor (m/f)
lo studente/la studentessa	student (m/f)
la rivista	magazine
l'ufficio	office

Extra Words

l'articolo	article
il datore di lavoro	employer

SMART TIP

Words ending in -ista like dentista (dentist), giornalista (journalist), regista (director), can be either masculine or feminine. You need to look at the article in order to tell.

CULTURE TIP

Some newspapers in Italy (especially regional ones) have the word giornale in the name: Il Giornale di Sicilia, Il Giornale di Sardegna. However the most important and national ones do not: La Repubblica, Il Corriere della Sera, La Stampa. The word telegiornale (combination of the word tele, abbreviated word for TV and giornale) is used to indicate the TV news.

Activity A

Fill in the blanks with the correct Italian word to complete the diary entry.

Caro diario,

Sono in una _____.
                    classroom

_____ sta parlando di un articolo sul
   The teacher

giornale. Ci sono molti _____ nella
                            students

mia classe. Non voglio stare qui. Vorrei essere una

_____ per una _____.
   journalist   magazine

Non mi piace essere una _____.
                              student

Activity B

Label each picture with the appropriate Italian words and articles.

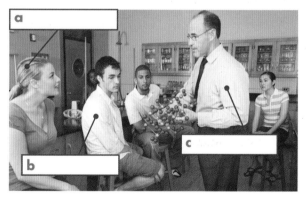

a

b

c

a

La Repubblica

b

c

Smart Phrases

Core Phrases

Qual è la sua professione? — What's your profession?
Faccio il/la giornalista. — I'm a journalist. (m/f)
Faccio il professore/ la professoressa. — I'm a teacher/professor. (m/f)
Che cosa vuole fare? — What do you want to do?
Voglio fare il professore/ la professoressa. — I want to be a teacher/ professor. (m/f)

Extra Phrases

Ci vediamo lunedì. — See you on Monday.
È assunto/assunta. — You're hired. (m/f)

Activity A

Qual è la sua professione? Look at the pictures and complete the sentences to tell the person's profession.

1 Faccio _____   2 Faccio _____

Che cosa vuole fare? Now look at the pictures and decide what each person wants to be. Write the answer on the blanks below.

3 _____   4 _____

Activity B

What do you say if you want to…

1 …ask someone what he or she wants to be?
_____

2 …say you want to be a professor?
_____

3 …ask someone about his or her profession?
_____

4 …say you're a journalist?
_____

Your Turn

Imagine you are a journalist. You're meeting a professor for the first time. Tell her your current profession and ask about hers. Then use the words *stilista* (fashion designer), *scrittore/scrittrice* (writer) or *regista* (director) to tell her what you want to be.

Write your sentences for more practice.

_____
_____
_____
_____
_____
_____
_____
_____
_____
_____

LESSON 4
Smart Grammar

Past Tense with a Regular Past Participle

To form the past tense—or *passato prossimo*—use the present tense of *avere*...

io	ho
tu	hai
Lei	ha
lui/lei	ha
noi	abbiamo
voi	avete
loro	hanno

...before the past participle.

Past participle of regular *–are* verbs

For the past participle of regular *–are* verbs, drop the *–are* and add *–ato* to the end, for example: *Io ho lavorato.* I (have) worked. *Tu hai lavorato.* You (have) worked.

Past participle of regular *–ere* verbs

For the past participle of regular *–ere* verbs, drop the *–ere* and add *–uto* to the end, for example: *Lui ha venduto.* He (has) sold. *Noi abbiamo venduto.* We (have) sold.

Past participle of regular *-ire* verbs

For the past participle of regular *–ire* verbs, drop the *–ire* and add *–ito* to the end, for example: *Voi avete spedito.* You (have) sent. *Loro hanno spedito.* They (have) sent.

SMART TIP

The Italian *passato prossimo* corresponds to the English simple past or present perfect tense. Like the present perfect, it has two parts: a helping verb and a past participle. So *Ho mangiato* is either I ate or I have eaten. In this Unit, you will learn the *passato prossimo* with the helping verb *avere*. In Unit 10 you will learn the *passato prossimo* with the helping verb *essere*.

SMART TIP

Do you remember the verbs *sapere* and *conoscere* that you learned in Unit 8? In the *passato prossimo*, *sapere* means to find out and *conoscere* means to meet:

Ho saputo che Luca è svizzero. I found out that Luca is Swiss.

Ho conosciuto molte persone alla festa. I met many people at the party.

Activity A

Complete the sentences with the past tense of the verb.

1 Tu _____ otto ore ieri (yesterday).
   lavorare

2 Noi _____ molti libri il mese scorso (last month).
   vendere

3 L'anno scorso (last year), io _____ molte cartoline.
   spedire

4 Loro _____ la settimana scorsa (last week).
   lavorare

Activity B

Rewrite the following sentences in the past tense.

1 Io lavoro in un ufficio.

   _____

2 Tu vendi i vestiti.

   _____

3 Lei mangia il pollo.

   _____

4 Voi finite i compiti.

   _____

5 Mary impara l'italiano.

   _____

6 Noi spediamo molte cartoline dall'Italia.

   _____

LESSON 5

Modulo di assunzione

A Job Application

Giorgio is applying for *un posto di correttore di bozze* (proofreader position) at *La Stampa*. *Un giorno* (some day) he wants to be a journalist. Look at his *modulo di assunzione* (application form).

Modulo di assunzione

La Stampa

Giorgio	Mariani	Milano	10/05/1984
Nome	Cognome	Nato a	Data di nascita (GG/MM/AAAA)

Firenze	Via Leopardi 12	50121
Residenza	Via e numero civico di residenza	CAP

055 674532	gmariani@alice.it
Telefono	E-Mail

TITOLO DI STUDIO/UNIVERSITÀ/ANNO

Laurea in Giornalismo,
Università Statale di Milano, 2007

PRECEDENTI IMPIEGHI	DA	A
Impiegato, Banca Nazionale	2007	2008
Assistente editoriale per La Nazione	2008	2009

Perché desidera questo posto?

Perché un giorno voglio fare il giornalista.
Come assistente editoriale ho imparato
molto e ho scritto anche qualche articolo.

SMART TIP

To help you understand a text or a conversation:

- Remember to look for cognates—Italian words that are similar or the same in English. For example: *assistente, editoriale, residenza, articolo.*

- Look for roots of words you know. For example: You know that the words *giornalista* and *giornale* mean "journalist" and "newspaper." *Giornalismo*, used in the application, has the same root and means "journalism." *Lavoro* has the same root as the verb *lavorare* and it means "job" or "work."

Activity A

Complete the sentences with information from the application.

1. Giorgio is applying for a position as _____ _____.

2. He graduated from the University of Milan in _____.

3. His first job was at _____.

4. He worked as _____.

5. At his previous job he also wrote _____.

Your Turn

The verb *scrivere* has an irregular past participle. Can you look in the job application and find it?

_____

SMART TIP

Perché is the equivalent of both why and because. Examples: *Perché desidera lavorare qui?* (Why do you want to work here?) *Voglio lavorare qui perché mi interessa la storia* (I want to work here because I'm interested in history).

LESSON 6 — Words to Know

Core Words

l'assistente	assistant
l'capoufficio/la capoufficio	office manager (m/f)
l'impiegato/l'impiegata	employee (m/f)
il lavoro	job
il segretario/la segretaria	secretary (m/f)
lo stipendio	salary

Extra Words

gli affari	business
l'azienda	company
difficile	difficult
facile	easy
molto	a lot

Activity A

Circle the word that best answers each question.

1 Which word is not a type of job?

   a **assistente**   b **impiegato**   c **stipendio**

2 Which word doesn't change its ending in the feminine form?

   a **assistente**   b **impiegato**   c **segretario**

3 Which person supervises the office?

   a **segretario**   b **capoufficio**   c **impiegato**

4 What do you call the amount of money you get paid for your work?

   a **impiegato**   b **stipendio**   c **lavoro**

Activity B

Read the clues and complete the crossword with vocabulary from the Core Words.

Across

5 Una persona che aiuta (helps).

6 Questa persona organizza (organizes) le cose in ufficio. (m)

Down

1 I soldi per il mio lavoro.

2 Questa persona lavora in ufficio. (m)

3 Sono giornalista. È il mio _____.

4 Lavora per me. È il mio _____.

Your Turn

Imagine you have your own *azienda*. Create a list of the people you need to hire. How many *impiegati*? How many of those will be *assistenti* and *segretari*? What is the *stipendio* for each *impiegato*?

Smart Phrases

Core Phrases

Perché desidera questo posto?	Why do you want this this position?
Perché voglio fare il giornalista.	Because I want to be a journalist.
Mi piace aiutare.	I like to help.
Mi piace scrivere.	I like to write.
Per quanto tempo ha lavorato là?	How long have you worked there?
Ho lavorato là per tre mesi.	I have worked there for three months.
è più facile di	it's easier than
è più difficile di	it's harder than

Extra Phrases

è pagato di più	it paid more
è pagato di meno	it paid less

SMART TIP

To say what activities you like, use *mi piace* and add a verb in the infinitive form. For example: *Mi piace giocare a calcio* (I like to play soccer), *Mi piace cantare* (I like to sing), *Mi piace leggere* (I like to read).

Activity A

ingegnere	**engineer**
avvocato	**lawyer**
costruttore	**builder**

What do you think? Write *più facile* or *più difficile* to compare each pair of jobs.

1 Il lavoro del dottore è _____ del lavoro del dentista.

2 Il lavoro del professore è _____ del lavoro dell'ingegnere.

3 Il lavoro del giornalista è _____ del lavoro dell'avvocato.

4 Il lavoro del costruttore è _____ del lavoro dello stilista.

Activity B

What do you say if you want to...

1 ...ask someone why he or she wants to be a journalist?

_____

_____

2 ...tell someone you like to help?

_____

_____

3 ...ask someone how long he or she has worked somewhere?

_____

_____

4 ...tell someone that you have worked somewhere for two years?

_____

_____

LESSON 8

Smart Grammar

Irregular Past Participles of Verbs Conjugated with *Avere*

Some verbs have irregular past participles; these must be memorized. Here is a list of the most common:

aprire	(ho) aperto	(I have) opened
bere	(ho) bevuto	(I have) drunk
chiudere	(ho) chiuso	(I have) closed
dire	(ho) detto	(I have) said/told
fare	(ho) fatto	(I have) done
leggere	(ho) letto	(I have) read
prendere	(ho) preso	(I have) taken
rispondere	(ho) risposto	(I have) answered
scrivere	(ho) scritto	(I have) written
vedere	(ho) visto	(I have) seen

Examples:

Luisa ha fatto i compiti.	Luisa did/has done the homework.
Ho aperto la porta.	I (have) opened the door.
Abbiamo scritto una lettera.	We wrote/have written a letter.

Activity A

Choose among the verbs in the list below and complete the following sentences in the *passato prossimo*.

> **aprire   chiudere   fare   vedere   bere   scrivere**
> **rispondere   prendere   leggere   dire**

1 Io _____ un bel film.

2 Noi _____ molti libri.

3 Ieri Laura _____ un bicchiere di vino rosso.

4 Loro _____ qualche lettera.

5 Tu _____ i compiti.

SMART PRONUNCIATION

In Italian double consonants are pronounced with more emphasis: *fatto, scritto, letto,* etc. This is particularly important because some words with double consonants have a different meaning than those with single consonants. Examples: *Casa* is house/home but *cassa* can be a case or cash register. *Sete* means thirst but *sette* is the number.

Use of *Da* and *Per* with Time Expressions

To specify how long you did something that you don't do anymore, use the *passato prossimo* with *per*. The question would be: *Per quanto tempo?* For how long? For example: *Per quanto tempo ha lavorato come impiegato? Ho lavorato come impiegato per tre anni.*

If you are still doing something that started in the past, use the present with *da*. The question would be: *Da quanto tempo?* How long? Example: *Da quanto tempo studia l'inglese? Studio l'inglese da cinque anni.*

Activity B

For each of the following sentences, indicate if the action is *conclusa* (completed) or *non conclusa*.

1 Ho studiato tedesco per due mesi.

  _____

2 Faccio l'ingegnere da 10 anni.

  _____

3 Ieri ho giocato a calcio per 2 ore.

  _____

4 Suono il piano dalle dieci.

  _____

Your Turn

Can you say how long you have been studying Italian?

  _____
  _____
  _____
  _____
  _____

Unit 9 Review

Activity A

Use the clues to complete the crossword puzzle. If the answer is a noun, be sure to include the correct definite article.

ACROSS

2 teacher (f)
4 magazine
5 salary

DOWN

1 secretary (m)
2 student (m)
3 office manager (m)

Activity B

Look at the subject of each answer and then complete the questions and the answers using the correct past tense conjugation for each verb.

1 Quando (lavorare) _____?

Noi _____ ieri.

2 Quando (leggere) il libro _____?

Io _____ il libro il mese scorso.

3 Perché non (mangiare) la pasta _____?

Lei non _____ la pasta perché non le piace.

Activity C

Complete the following sentences with the correct irregular past participle.

1 Io ho (aprire) _____ la porta (the door).
2 Laura ha (rispondere) _____ al telefono.
3 Loro hanno (dire) _____ la verità (the truth).
4 Carlo ha (prendere) _____ il treno per Bologna.
5 Voi avete (vedere) _____ un film italiano.

Activity D

The following sentences contain a mistake. Rewrite them to correct the mistakes.

1 Che cosa avete mangiato domani?

_____

2 Studio l'italiano per due anni.

_____

3 L'anno scorso scrivo un articolo per *La Repubblica*.

_____

4 Io e Laura ho fatto molte cose.

_____

Challenge

Can you tell the cognates for these two Italian professions?

poliziotto _____

architetto_____

Internet Activity

Go to **www.berlitzbooks.com/5minute** for a list of Italian-language job search engines to browse. How many *impiegato* positions can you find? What about *segretari* and *avvocati*? What are the *requisiti* (requirements) for each position?

88   Unit 9   Professions

At Home/Going Out

In this unit you will:
- talk about things to do around a house or an apartment.
- use the imperative form to give orders and instructions.
- use expressions for going out at night.
- use vocabulary about places to go.
- learn the past tense of verbs with the auxiliary *essere*.

LESSON 1

Aiutami!

Elisa's E-mail

Elisa writes an e-mail to her brother Matteo. She asks him to help her clean her apartment. (Notice how they are using the informal because they are related.)

```
○ ○ ○
Data:     martedì 26 agosto
Da:       Elisa
A:        Matteo
Oggetto:  Aiutami!

Ciao Matteo,
puoi aiutarmi a pulire il mio
appartamento? Papà e mamma arrivano
domani e l'appartamento è un po' in
disordine. Voglio spolverare, prendere
le cose da terra e sistemare i vestiti
nell'armadio. Poi voglio pulire le
stanze e imbiancare la mia camera da
letto. Come puoi aiutarmi? Tu spolveri
e io sistemo l'armadio. Poi, puliamo e
imbianchiamo insieme.
Aiutami per favore!
Un abbraccio,
Elisa
```

in disordine	messy	da terra	from the floor
pulire	to clean	imbiancare	to paint
Non ti preoccupare!	Don't worry!	spolverare	to dust
		insieme	together
prendere	to pick up		

Activity A
Circle the correct answer for each question.

1 What does Elisa need help with?
   a her house   **b her apartment**

2 Who will visit Elisa tomorrow?
   a her parents   **b her aunt and uncle**

3 What does Elisa ask Matteo to do?
   a organize her closet   **b dust**

4 What does Elisa suggest they do together?
   a organize her closet   **b paint**

Activity B
Read Matteo's response. Then answer the questions in Italian.

```
○ ○ ○
Data:     martedì 26 agosto
Da:       Matteo
A:        Elisa
Oggetto:  Aiutami!

Ciao Elisa,
sì, posso aiutarti. Però non voglio
spolverare. Tu spolveri e io sistemo
l'armadio. Poi, puliamo e imbianchiamo
insieme.
Non ti preoccupare! Ti aiuto.
A presto,
Matteo
```

1 Is Matteo going to help Elisa?
_____

2 What doesn't Matteo want to do?
_____

3 What does Matteo want to do?
_____

4 What does Matteo say that he and Elisa can do together?
_____

Words to Know

Core Words

l'appartamento	apartment
l'armadio	armoire/wardrobe
il bagno	bathroom
la camera/stanza	room
la camera da letto	bedroom
la cucina	kitchen
la sala da pranzo	dining room
il soggiorno	living room

Extra Words

la finestra	window
il giardino	garden
il pavimento	floor
le scale	stairs

Activity A

Fill in the blanks with the correct Italian words to complete the dialogue. For the *io* part of the dialogue, answer the questions based on your own home.

Amico Abiti in una casa o in _____ ?
an apartment

Io Abito in _____ .

Amico Quante _____ ci sono?
rooms

Io Ci sono _____ .

Amico Quali sono _____ più grandi?
the rooms

Io Le camere più grandi sono _____

_____ .

Activity B

Look at each picture. Then choose the correct word from the box to name each picture.

| il bagno | la camera da letto | il soggiorno |
| la cucina | la sala da pranzo | l'armadio |

1 _____   2 _____

3 _____   4 _____

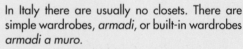

5 _____   6 _____

CULTURE TIP

In Italy there are usually no closets. There are simple wardrobes, *armadi*, or built-in wardrobes *armadi a muro.*

CULTURE TIP

In Italy, the first floor corresponds to the American second floor and it is called *pianterreno*. So start counting from the level above the street: *primo piano, secondo piano*, etc.

LESSON 3

Smart Phrases

Core Phrases

Puoi aiutarmi?	Can you help me?
Sì, posso aiutarti.	Yes, I can help you.
No, non posso aiutarti.	No, I can't help you.
Cosa vuoi che faccia?	What do you want me to do?
Subito.	Right away.

Extra Phrases

Aiutami per favore!	Help me please!
Un abbraccio.	Hugs.

SMART TIP

Did you notice the informal "you" was used in the phrases above? That's because the correspondence in Lesson 1 was between siblings. Remember to use the formal when speaking to all but family, friends and children.

Activity A

What do you say if you want to…

1 …ask someone to help you?

_____

2 …say that you can't help someone?

_____

3 …ask what someone wants you to do?

_____

4 …say "right away"?

_____

Activity B

Put the dialogue in order. Number the phrases 1–4.

> Sì, posso aiutarti. Cosa vuoi che faccia?

\#

> Sistema i vestiti!

\#

> Subito.

\#

> Puoi aiutarmi?

\#

Smart Grammar

Commands

Italian commands are verb forms used to give an order. Following are the most common command forms for –are, -ere and –ire verbs.

aiutare	to help
(tu) Aiuta!	Help! (sing., inf.)
(Lei) Aiuti!	Help! (sing., form.)
(noi) Aiutiamo!	Let's help!
(voi) Aiutate!	Help! (pl.)

prendere	to pick up
(tu) Prendi!	Pick up! (sing., inf.)
(Lei) Prenda!	Pick up! (sing., form.)
(noi) Prendiamo!	Let's pick up!
(voi) Prendete!	Pick up! (pl.)

pulire	to clean
(tu) Pulisci!	Clean! (sing., inf.)
(Lei) Pulisca!	Clean! (sing., form.)
(noi) Puliamo!	Let's clean!
(voi) Pulite!	Clean! (pl.)

SMART TIP

When giving a command, remember to drop the pronoun since the verb form indicates the person spoken to. Note that the *tu* (except with -are verbs), *noi* and *voi* command forms are the same as the present tense that you already know. The *Lei* form is different.

Activity A

Paola needs to get things done around the house. She asks her family to help out. Use the given verbs and nouns to write each command.

(1) imbiancare/ la stanza (2) sistemare/ l'armadio (3) pulire/ il pavimento

The verb *potere* (may, can, to be able)

The verb *potere* is irregular. The chart shows its conjugation in the present tense. Remember that *potere* is usually followed by an infinitive.

io	posso	I can
tu	puoi	you can
Lei	può	you can
lui/lei	può	he/she can
noi	possiamo	we can
voi	potete	you can
loro	possono	they can

Activity B

Paola used commands to get things done. Now use *potere* to make those commands more polite.

1 _____ imbiancare la stanza?
2 _____ sistemare l'armadio?
3 _____ pulire il pavimento?

Dove sei stato?

Diary Entry

Read Silvana's diary entry about where she went this week.

> Caro diario,
>
> questa è stata una bella settimana.
> L'altro ieri io e i miei amici siamo stati
> a un concerto di musica rock. Ci siamo
> divertiti molto. Ieri io e mia madre siamo
> andate a comprare dei vestiti. Poi sono
> andata in discoteca con il mio ragazzo
> e abbiamo ballato tutta la notte. Voglio
> andare a ballare di nuovo molto presto.

ci siamo divertiti	we had fun
tutta la notte	all night
di nuovo	again
molto presto	very soon

Activity A
Circle the correct answer for each question.

1 What did Silvana do the day before yesterday?
   a went to the concert   **b** went to the club

2 What did Silvana do yesterday?
   a went to the concert   **b** went to the store

3 What did Silvana do last night?
   a went to the club   **b** went to the concert

4 What does Silvana want to do again?
   a buy clothes   **b** dance

Activity B
Answer the following questions in Italian.

1 How has Silvana's week been?
_____

2 How was the concert the other day?
_____

3 Where were Silvana and her friends the day before yesterday?
_____

4 Whom did she go with?
_____

Activity C
Write in Italian what Silvana did each day.

1 l'altro ieri
_____

2 ieri
_____

3 ieri sera
_____

CULTURE TIP

Unlike English, the word *notte* (night) is used only for hours after midnight till around 3:00 AM. Use *sera* (evening) between 7:00 PM and 11:00 PM.

LESSON 6

Words to Know

Core Words

ieri	yesterday
ieri sera	last night
l'altro ieri	day before yesterday
la settimana scorsa	last week
ballare	to dance
il cinema	movie theater
il concerto	concert
la discoteca	club
il film	movie
il teatro	theater

Activity A

Where did the following people go last night? Look at the pictures and write the Italian word for the place where each person went.

1 _____

2 _____

3 _____

4 _____

Activity B

Oggi è mercoledì. Write *ieri sera, ieri, l'altro ieri o la settimana scorsa* to tell when you did each activity.

1   Io ho ballato martedì. _____

2   Sono andato al cinema lunedì. _____

3   Sono stato al concerto mercoledì scorso. _____

4   Sono andato a teatro martedì sera. _____

Activity C

Complete the crossword puzzle in Italian using the English clue words. Be sure to include the definite article, when needed.

ACROSS

1 theater
4 movie theater
5 last night
6 movie

DOWN

2 day before yesterday
3 to dance

> **SMART TIP**
>
> The word for movie theater is *cinema*. Remember that it is a masculine word even though it ends in *a* and it doesn't change in the plural. So you will say: *un cinema, due cinema.*

LESSON 7

Smart Phrases

Core Phrases

Che cosa hai fatto ieri sera/ieri/l'altro ieri/ la settimana scorsa?	What did you do last night/ yesterday/the day before yesterday/last week?
Che cosa vuoi fare?	What do you want to do?
Voglio stare a casa.	I want to stay in.
Voglio uscire.	I want to go out.

Extra Phrases

Andiamo a bere qualcosa!	Let's have a drink!
Usciamo!	Let's go out!

Activity A

What do you say if you want to…

1 …ask what someone did last week?

_____

2 …ask what someone wants to do?

_____

3 …say you want to go out?

_____

4 …say you want to stay in?

_____

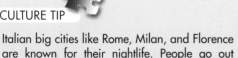

CULTURE TIP

Italian big cities like Rome, Milan, and Florence are known for their nightlife. People go out to dinner as late as 10 PM depending on the region and the season and stay out all night long. Often, clubs don't open until midnight and stay open until dawn.

Activity B

Roberto wants to take Silvia out tonight. Silvia doesn't want to go out. Roberto suggests activities, but to no avail. Put their dialogue in order to figure out what Roberto decides to do. (Notice Roberto uses the informal because Silvia is his friend.)

___	**Roberto**	Ma io voglio uscire di casa. Vuoi andare a ballare?
___	**Silvia**	Sono andata al cinema ieri sera.
___	**Roberto**	Andiamo al cinema?
___	**Silvia**	Voglio stare a casa stasera.
___	**Roberto**	Va bene, stiamo a casa stasera.
___	**Silvia**	Sono andata a ballare con i miei amici ieri.
_1_	**Roberto**	Che cosa vuoi fare stasera?

Write in Italian what Roberto ultimately decides to do about the evening.

_____

_____

_____

_____

_____

Your Turn

Che cosa vuole fare stasera?

_____

_____

_____

_____

LESSON 8

Smart Grammar

Past tense of verbs with *essere*

The verb *andare* takes *essere* as its helping verb and must agree in gender and number like an adjective. See the conjugation below.

Verbs that take *essere* are usually verbs of motion. You already know how to form regular past participles (see Unit 9). Some verbs that take *essere* have irregular past participles. Here are some of the most common:

essere	(sono) stato/a	(I have) been
venire	(sono) venuto/a	(I have) come
nascere	(sono) nato/a	(I was) born
rimanere	(sono) rimasto/a	(I have) stayed

io	sono	andato/a	I went/have gone
tu	sei	andato/a	you went/have gone
Lei	è	andato/a	you went/have gone
lui/lei	è	andato/a	he/she went/has gone
noi	siamo	andati/e	we went/have gone
voi	siete	andati/e	you went/have gone
loro	sono	andati/e	they went/have gone

Examples:

Lei è andata al negozio.   She went/has been to the store.

Noi siamo rimasti a casa.   We (have) stayed home.

Activity A

Insert the correct ending—pay attentión to the agreement!

1   Luisa è andat _____ al supermercato.

2   Marco è stat _____ in Italia l'anno scorso.

3   Quelle ragazze sono nat _____ in Italia.

4   Noi siamo rimast _____ a casa ieri sera.

Activity B

Choose a verb from the list and complete each sentence using the past tense.

> nascere   andare   rimanere   venire

1   Io _____ a casa ieri.

2   Mio nonno _____ il 2 giugno 1930.

3   Giulia e Paola _____ al cinema ieri sera.

4   Marcello e Luigi _____ a trovarmi (to visit me) dopo la lezione.

Activity C

Now see if you can translate the sentences in Activity B. Write the English version of the sentences on the lines provided.

1   _____

2   _____

3   _____

4   _____

Your Turn

Dov'è nato/nata?

_____

Dov'è andato/andata ieri sera?

_____

Unit 10 Review

Activity A

Solve the following anagrams. Use the pictures as clues.

1 b g n o a  _ _ _ _ _

2 l i m f _ _ _ _

3 b l r l a r e a _ _ _ _ _ _ _

4 r i b i a c a m e n _ _ _ _ _ _ _ _ _

5 i u n c c a _ _ _ _ _ _

Activity B

Circle the sentence that best completes Stefania's answers.

1 **Giorgio** Che cosa vuoi fare stasera?

Stefania Sono stanca.

  a Ho visto la televisione ieri sera.   **b Voglio stare a casa stasera.**

2 **Giorgio** Voglio uscire! Andiamo a ballare.

Stefania No Giorgio.

  a Sono andata a ballare con Luigi ieri.   **b Sono andata al cinema ieri sera.**

3 **Giorgio** Vuoi una birra?

Stefania No grazie.

  a Voglio uscire.   **b Ho bevuto una birra questo pomeriggio.**

4 **Giorgio** Possiamo andare al cinema stasera.

Stefania No.

  a Non voglio uscire stasera.   **b Che cosa hai fatto ieri sera?**

Activity C

Change the following sentences into the past tense. Remember to use the helping verb *essere*.

1 Oggi rimango a casa.

_____

2 Vai al cinema dopo cena?

_____

3 Silvia e Paola vanno al supermercato.

_____

4 Paola è in Italia.

_____

Activity D

Write the imperative forms of the following questions.

1 Puoi aiutare la mamma in cucina?

_____

2 Potete sistemare la vostra camera?

_____

3 Può prendere le cose da terra?

_____

4 Possiamo imbiancare la camera?

_____

> **Challenge**
>
> Make two lists of verbs: one with verbs that require *avere* and one with verbs that require *essere* in the past. Then choose two verbs and conjugate them in the past tense.

Internet Activity

Go to **www.berlitzbooks.com/5minute** for a list of real estate web sites and choose a region (*regione*), a district (*provincia*) and a city (*comune*). Then write down what rooms you saw.

Unit 11 Body and Health

In this unit you will:
- learn vocabulary for body and health.
- use adverbs of time.
- describe common symptoms and ailments.
- conjugate regular verbs in the future.

LESSON 1

Sono malato

Dialogue

Maria asks her friend Roberto to play tennis, but he's sick. They make an appointment for a different day. Listen to their conversation.

Roberto Ciao Maria. Cosa fai oggi?

Maria Vado a giocare a tennis. Vuoi venire?

Roberto No, non posso giocare perché sono malato.

Maria Mi dispiace. Possiamo andare giovedì o venerdì.

Roberto Se sto meglio possiamo andare a giocare venerdì.

Maria Va bene. Chiamami venerdì e guarisci presto!

Activity A

Choose the correct answer for each question.

1 When is Maria going to play tennis?
   a today   **b tomorrow**

2 Why doesn't Roberto play with Maria?
   a He doesn't want to.   **b He can't.**

3 What other day is he going to play?
   a Thursday   **b Friday**

4 Who is going to call on Friday?
   a Maria   **b Roberto**

Activity B

On Friday, Roberto sends Maria a text message. Read his message and Maria's response, then answer the questions.

> Mi dispiace Maria ma non posso giocare oggi. Sono ancora malato. Andiamo a giocare domenica o lunedì?
> Roberto

> Che peccato! Non ti preoccupare. Chiamami domenica!
> Maria

1 Why can't Roberto play on Friday?
   a He's still sick.   **b He doesn't want to.**

2 What does Maria tell Roberto?
   a not to call her   **b not to worry**

3 When will they talk again?
   a Sunday   **b Monday**

Activity C

Today is Sunday. Write a text message from Roberto to Maria to tell her that he wants to play on Monday.

LESSON 2

Words to Know

Core Words

Gli sport (Sports)

il calcio	soccer
il ciclismo	cycling
il nuoto	swimming
la pallacanestro	basketball
la pallavolo	volleyball
il tennis	tennis

La salute (Health)

grasso/grassa	fat (m/f)
magro/magra	slender (m/f)
malato/malata	sick (m/f)
sano/sana	healthy (m/f)
la salute	health
stressato/stressata	stressed (m/f)
la palestra	gym
pesare	to weigh
il peso	weight

Activity A

Write the name of the sport under each picture.

1 _____

2 _____

3 _____

4 _____

Activity B

Fill in the blanks with the correct Italian word.

1 Dov'è _____?
   the gym

2 Qual è il suo _____?
   weight

3 Lui non vuole essere _____.
   fat

4 Lei mangia bene per rimanere _____
   slender

   e _____.
   healthy

5 Perché è _____?
   stressed

6 È _____ Roberto?
   sick

Activity C

Match the English word to the correct Italian translation.

1 slender
   a grasso   b magro

2 volleyball
   a la pallavolo b la pallacanestro

3 to weigh
   a pesare   b il peso

4 healthy
   a malato   b sano

SMART TIP

Did you notice that the words *pallacanestro* and *pallavolo* contain the word *palla* (ball)? *Pallacanestro* is formed with the words ball and basket (*canestro*), and *pallavolo* with the words ball and *volo* (from the verb to fly). The Italian words for handball and water polo follow a similar pattern: *pallamano, pallanuoto*.

LESSON 3

Smart Phrases

Core Phrases

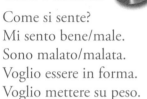

Come si sente?	How are you feeling?
Mi sento bene/male.	I am feeling well/bad.
Sono malato/malata.	I'm sick. (m/f)
Voglio essere in forma.	I want to be in shape.
Voglio mettere su peso.	I want to gain weight.
Voglio perdere peso.	I want to lose weight.

Extra Phrases

ancora	still
Che peccato!	What a shame!
Guarisci presto!	Get well soon!
Mi dispiace.	I'm sorry.

Activity A

What do you say if you want to…

1   …say you're feeling well?

_____

2   …say you want to be in shape?

_____

3   …ask how someone is feeling?

_____

4   …say you want to lose weight?

_____

Activity B

Choose the best phrase for each picture.

1

a Mi sento male.

b Mi sento bene.

2

a Voglio essere in forma.

b Sono malata.

3

a Voglio perdere peso.

b Mi sento bene.

4

a Voglio perdere peso.

b Voglio mettere su peso.

5

a Mi sento male.

b Sono in forma.

Your Turn

Come si sente? Now talk about how you feel. Then tell if you are in *forma* or need *perdere peso* or *mettere su peso.*

_____

_____

_____

LESSON 4

Smart Grammar

Regular Verbs in the Future Tense

To form the future tense, add the future endings -ò, -ai, -à, -emo, -ete, -anno to the infinitive form without the final -e. So, the future tense of the -ere verb vendere, to sell, is: io venderò, tu venderai, Lei venderà, lui/lei venderà, noi venderemo, voi venderete, loro venderanno. And, the future tense of the -ire verb, finire, to finish, is: io finirò, tu finirai, Lei finirà, lui/lei finirà, noi finiremo, voi finirete, loro finiranno.
For verbs ending in -are, the a changes into e first:

io lavorerò	I will work
tu lavorerai	you will work
Lei lavorerà	you will work
lui/lei lavorerà	he/she will work
noi lavoreremo	we will work
voi lavorerete	you will work
loro lavoreranno	they will work

Activity A

Write what each person will do. The personal pronoun and verb are provided for you.

1 lui, scrivere _____

2 io, ballare _____

3 loro, studiare _____

4 noi, partire _____

5 tu, conoscere _____

6 voi, correre _____

SMART TIPS

- Verbs ending in -care and -gare add an h in front of -er in order to retain the hard sound. So giocare will be giocherò, giocherai, giocherà, etc. Pagare will be pagherò, pagherai, pagherà, etc.
- Verbs in -ciare and -giare drop the i before the future endings. So the future of cominciare will be comincerò, comincerai, etc. The future of mangiare will be mangerò, mangerai, etc.
- Some verbs form the future with irregular stems but regular future endings. These are some of the most common:
  andare = andrò, andrai, ...   fare = farò, farai, ...
  avere = avrò, avrai, ...   potere = potrò, potrai, ...
  essere = sarò, sarai, ...   volere = vorrò, vorrai, ...

Activity B

Make each sentence a question. The first one is done for you.

1 Domani cucinerò il pollo.
   Quando cucinerai il pollo?

2 Noi studieremo per l'esame la settimana prossima.
   _____

3 Io correrò nel parco.
   _____

4 Noi balleremo in discoteca.
   _____

5 Io pulirò la mia stanza sabato.
   _____

6 Luisa scriverà una lettera.
   _____

Your Turn

Look at each picture and tell what is going to happen.

_____ _____

_____ _____

LESSON 5
La medicina

Medical Advertisement

Read the advertisement; remember to look for cognates and root words you know for help.

Medicina per il raffreddore

Combatte la febbre e la tosse.
Allevia il mal di testa e il mal di gola.
Dà benessere a tutto il corpo.
Non occorre una ricetta.

| allevia | alleviates |
| il corpo | the body |

Activity A
Choose the correct answer for each question.

1 What is this ad for?
   a cold medicine   b pain medicine
2 What does the medicine help with?
   a fever   b broken foot
3 What does the medicine alleviate?
   a toothaches   b headaches
4 Why don't you need to see a doctor to get this medicine?
   a You don't need a prescription.   b You don't need a shot.

Read the advertisement; remember to look for cognates and root words you know for help.

Medicina per la tosse

Combatte il mal di gola.
Allevia la febbre, elimina il mal di testa.
Prendere due volte al giorno.
Vi sentirete meglio subito.
Occorre una ricetta.

Activity B
Choose the correct answer for each question.

1 What is this ad for?
   a stomach medicine b cough medicine
2 What does the medicine help with?
   a headaches   b sore throat
3 What does the medicine alleviate?
   a fever   b toothache
4 How often should you take this medicine?
   a every day   b twice a day
5 Do you need to see a doctor to get this medicine?
   a yes   b no

Activity C
Complete the following sentences to compare both medicines.

La medicina per il raffreddore combatte _____ e la medicina _____ combatte _____. Le due medicine alleviano _____. La medicina per la tosse allevia _____ e _____ per il raffreddore allevia _____.

CULTURE TIP

When looking for a pharmacy in Italy, look for the lit up green cross. Pharmacists are expected to give pharmaceutical advice as a part of their job and are there to help you. If you have any questions before going to a doctor, you can head to a pharmacist for medical advice. If a pharmacy is closed, you will find on display the names of the *farmacie di turno* (pharmacies on duty) where you can go.

Words to Know

Core Words

il mal di denti	toothache
il mal di gola	sore throat
il mal di pancia	stomachache
il mal di testa	headache
la febbre	fever
il raffreddore	cold
la tosse	cough
il dentista/la dentista	dentist (m/f)
il dottore/la dottoressa	doctor (m/f)
l'iniezione	shot
la medicina	medicine
l'ospedale	hospital
la ricetta	prescription

Activity A

You have various ailments. Circle the word that best completes the sentence.

1 Hai la tosse. Hai bisogno di _____.

   a un dentista   **b una medicina**

2 Hai mal di denti. Vai _____.

   a all'ospedale   **b dal dentista**

3 Hai la febbre. Il dottore ti dà _____.

   a un'iniezione   **b una ricetta**

4 Hai mal di testa. Hai bisogno di _____.

   a una medicina   **b un'iniezione**

5 Hai mal di gola. Vai _____.

   a dal dentista   **b dal dottore**

Activity B

The following people are not feeling well. Look at the pictures and write the corresponding ailments.

1 _____

2 _____

3 _____

4 _____

Your Turn

Lei è un dottore/una dottoressa. Talk about your patient. *Che cos'ha? Di cosa ha bisogno?*

_____

_____

_____

_____

CULTURE TIP

Italy has the largest number of *terme*, natural spas, thanks to the many mineral springs and volcanic areas in the country. The tradition of visiting *le terme* to help alleviate illness comes from ancient Rome; today, spas are not only visited for illness but also for relaxation purposes. Spas in Abano, Merano, Salsomaggiore, Chianciano, Montecatini and Ischia are among the most famous.

LESSON 7
Smart Phrases

Core Phrases

Che cosa le fa male?	What hurts?
Mi fa male il braccio.	My arm hurts.
Mi fanno male le gambe.	My legs hurt.
Mi fa male la mano.	My hand hurts.
Mi fanno male i piedi.	My feet hurt.
Mi fa male la schiena.	My back hurts.

Extra Phrases

Può raccomandarmi un dottore/dentista?	Can you recommend a doctor/dentist?
Deve andare da un dottore/dentista.	You need to see a doctor/dentist.

SMART TIPS

- When talking about body parts in Italian don't use possessive adjectives such as *il mio/la mia/le mie/i miei* (my) as in English. Instead, use the definite article *il/lo/la*, etc., and the idiomatic expression *mi fa male* (sing.) or *mi fanno male* (pl.), to hurt. For example: *Mi fa male il braccio* literally means "The arm hurts me."

- The verb *dovere* is used to express obligation or necessity. It's an irregular *–ere* verb and is often translated as "to have to," "must" or "need to." For example: *Devi andare dal dottore* (You need to go to a doctor's).

Activity A

Look at each picture and complete each sentence.

1   Mi fa male _____

2   Le fa male _____

3   Mi fanno male _____

4   Gli fa male _____

Activity B

You are waiting to see the doctor. Tell the *infermiere/infermiera* (nurse, m/f) how you feel. Then tell him/her your symptoms.

Choose words or phrases from the box to write your description.

> **malato/malata**   **braccio**   **mi fa male la schiena**
> **febbre**   **mi fa male il braccio**   **ho mal di testa**

_____
_____
_____
_____
_____

Activity C

Write *la relazione dell'infermiere/infermiera* (the nurse's report) based on what you told her in Activity B. Use *gli/le* instead of *mi*.

_____
_____
_____

LESSON 8
Smart Grammar

Adverbs of Time

Use the following words when talking about how frequently something happens.

di solito	usually
non … mai	never
ogni giorno	every day
qualche volta	sometimes
sempre	always
spesso	often
una volta/due volte	once/twice

Examples

Gioco spesso a tennis.	I play soccer often.
Di solito Roberto corre il sabato.	Usually Roberto runs on Saturdays.

> **SMART TIP**
>
> Note that *sempre* and *spesso* are usually placed after the verb. *Mai* has the following construction: *non + verb + mai*. Example: *Maria non fa mai ginnastica* (Maria never does gymnastics).

Activity A

Choose the word that best describes how often you do these activities or how often this happens to you.

1 Vado dal dottore.
a spesso   **b qualche volta**   **c mai**

2 Vado in palestra.
a spesso   **b qualche volta**   **c mai**

3 Gioco a tennis due volte alla settimana.
a spesso   **b qualche volta**   **c mai**

4 Faccio ginnastica la domenica.
a spesso   **b qualche volta**   **c mai**

Activity B

Translate these sentences from English to Italian. If you need help with prepositions, look at the Smart Tip on page 74.

1 I sometimes play volleyball.

_____

2 I always go to the gym.

_____

3 I am usually stressed.

_____

4 I play tennis once a week.

_____

5 I never go to the doctor.

_____

6 I run every day.

_____

Activity C

Now translate these questions.

1 Do you always go to Italy in July?

_____

2 Do you usually travel during the summer?

_____

3 Does Massimo eat lunch at home every day?

_____

Your Turn

In Italian, tell what you do or don't do in these time frames.

1 ogni giorno _____

2 qualche volta _____

3 mai _____

4 di solito _____

Activity A

I fratelli Carlo e Marina don't agree on anything. Carlo will say something and Marina will immediately say the opposite or something else. Fill in Marina's half of the dialogue with the appropriate Italian phrases.

Carlo Mi sento male.

Marina _____
I feel good.

Carlo Ho mal di testa.

Marina _____
I never have an headache.

Carlo La settimana prossima andrò dal dentista.

Marina _____
I'm not going to the dentist's.

Carlo Ho mal di denti.

Marina _____
I have a stomachache.

Carlo Voglio andare dal dottore.

Marina _____
I don't want to go to the doctor.

Carlo Faccio ginnastica perché voglio rimanere in forma.

Marina _____
I exercise because I want to lose weight.

Activity B

What's wrong with these sentences? Rewrite them so that they are grammatically correct.

1 Mi fanno male la testa. _____

2 Mi fa male il mio braccio. _____

3 Vado mai in palestra. _____

4 Sempre Teresa corre nel parco.
   _____

5 Laura cucinerò domani. _____

6 Mi fa male i piedi. _____

Activity C

Use the pictures as clues to unscramble the anagrams. You will create words you learned in this unit.

1 i l c o m s i c
   _ _ _ _ _ _ _ _

2 s n e n t i
   _ _ _ _ _ _

3 a m l i d e t s a t
   _ _ _   _ _
   _ _ _ _ _

4 a n i i c d e m
   _ _ _ _ _ _ _ _

5 b r b e f e
   _ _ _ _ _ _

6 a s t i t e n d
   _ _ _ _ _ _ _ _

Challenge

Answer the following questions based on your life.

Chi cucinerà domani? _____

Che fa di solito per divertirsi? _____

Che farà la settimana prossima? _____

Internet Activity

Go to **www.berlitzbooks.com/5minute** for a list of websites for gyms in Italy. Select a gym, then find out what the gym offers. What kinds of memberships are available? What are the facilities like? Are there exercise classes?

A

l'abbigliamento	lah·bee·llyah·mehn·toh	clothing
l'acqua	lah·kwah	water
l'aereo	lah·eh·reh·oh	plane
l'aeroporto	lah·eh·roh·pohr·toh	airport
agosto	ah·goh·stoh	August
l'altro ieri	lahl·troh yeh·ree	day before yesterday adv
amare	ah·mah·reh	to love
all'angolo	ah·lahn·goh·loh	on the corner
l'anno	lah·noh	year
americano/	ah·may·ree·kah·noh/	American m/f
americana	ah·may·ree·kah·nah	
gli animali	lly ah·nee·mah·lee	animals
aprile	ah·pree·leh	April
l'appartamento	lah·pahr·tah·mayn·toh	apartment, flat BE
l'armadio	lahr·mah·dyoh	armoire/wardrobe
arrivederci	ahr·ree·veh·dehr·chee	goodbye
l'assegno	lah·say·nyoh	check n, cheque BE
l'assistente	lah·see·stehn·teh	assistant m/f
Australia	ow·strah·lyah	Australia
australiano/	ow·strah·lyah·noy/	Australian m/f
australiana	ow·strah·lyah·nah	
l'autobus	low·toy·boos	bus
l'autunno	low·too·noh	autumn, fall

B

ballare	bah·lah·reh	dance v
la bambina	lah bahm·bee·nah	(young) girl, child
il bambino	eel bahm·bee·noy	(young) boy, child
i bagagli	ee bah·gah·llee	luggage
il bagno	eel bah·nyoh	bathroom
la banca	lah bahn·kah	bank
il bancomat	eel bahn·koh·maht	debit card
bello/bella	beh·loh/beh·lah	nice m/f
bere	beh·reh	drink v
le bevande	leh beh·vahn·deh	drinks
bianco/bianca	byahn·koh/byahn·kah	white m/f
la biblioteca	lah bee·blyoh·teh·kah	library

il biglietto	eel bee·llyeh·toh	ticket
la birra	lah bee·rah	beer
la bistecca	lah bees·teh·kah	steak
blu	bloo	blue

C

il caffè	eel kah·feh	coffee
il calcio	eel kahl·chyoh	soccer
caldo	kahl·doh	warm (temperature)
i calzini	ee kahl·tsee·nee	socks
la camera	lah kah·meh·rah	room
la camera	lah kah·meh·rah	bedroom
da letto	dah leh·toh	
la camicia	lah kah·mee·chyah	shirt
Canada	kah·nah·dah	Canada
canadese	kah·nah·day·say	Canadian
il cane	eel kah·neh	dog
il capoufficio/	eel kah·poh·oo·fee·chyoh/	office manager m/f
la capoufficio	lah kah·poh·oo·fee·chyoh	
il cappotto	eel kah·poh·toh	coat
la carne	lah kahr·neh	meat
la carta	lah kahr·tah	credit card
di credito	dee cray·dee·toh	
la casa	lah kah·sah	house
celibe	cheh·lee·beh	single m
la chiesa	lah kyeh·zah	church
il cibo	eel chee·boh	food
il ciclismo	eel chee·klees·moh	cycling
ciao	chyah·oh	hello/goodbye
cinquanta	cheen·kwahn·tah	50
cinque	cheen·kweh	5
il cinema	eel chee·neh·mah	movie theater, cinema BE
la classe	lah klah·seh	classroom
la colazione	lah koh·lah·tsyoh·neh	breakfast
i colori	ee koh·loh·ree	colors
il compleanno	eel kohm·pleh·ah·noh	birthday
il concerto	eel kohn·chehr·toh	concert
i contanti	ee kohn·tahn·tee	cash
il costume	eel koh·stoo·meh	bathing suit

adj	adjective	adv	adverb	BE	British English

n	noun	v	verb

la cravatta	lah krah·vah·tah	tie (clothing)
la cucina	lah koo·chee·nah	kitchen
il cugino/	eel koo·jee·noh/	cousin m/f
la cugina	lah koo·jee·nah	

D

davanti	dah·vahn·tee	in front
il dentista/	eel dehn·tee·stah/	dentist m/f
la dentista	lah dehn·tee·stah	
a destra	ah deh·strah	to the right
dicembre	dee·chehm·breh	December
diciassette	dyah·chyah·seh·teh	17
diciannove	dee·chyah·noh·veh	19
diciotto	dee·chyoh·toh	18
dieci	dyeh·chee	10
dietro	dyeh·troh	behind
la discoteca	lah dee·skoh·teh·kah	club
dodici	doh·dee·chee	12
domenica	doh·meh·nee·kah	Sunday
la donna	lah doh·nah	woman
il dottore	eel doh·toh·reh	doctor m
la dottoressa	lah doh·toh·reh·sah	doctor f
due	dweh	2

E

l'edificio	lay·dee·fee·chyoh	building
l'estate	leh·stah·teh	summer

F

la famiglia	lah fah·mee·llyah	family
febbraio	feh·brah·yoh	February
la febbre	lah feh·breh	fever, temperature
la fermata	lah fehr·mah·tah	bus stop
dell'autobus	deh·low·toh·boos	
i figli	ee fee·lly	children

la figlia	lah fee·llyah	daughter
il figlio	eel fee·llyoh	son
il film	eel feelm	movie
il formaggio	eel fohr·mah·jyoh	cheese
fra	frah	between
i fratelli	ee frah·teh·lee	brothers/siblings
il fratello	eel frah·teh·loh	brother
freddo	fray·doh	cold, cool (temperature)
la frutta	lah froo·tah	fruit

G

il gatto	eel gah·toy	cat
i genitori	ee jeh·nee·toh·ree	parents
il gelato	eel jeh·lah·toh	ice cream
gennaio	jeh·nah·yoh	January
la giacca	lah jyah·kah	jacket
giallo/gialla	jyah·loh/jyah·lah	yellow m/f
il giornale	eel jyohr·nah·leh	newspaper
il giornalista/	eel jyohr·nah·lee·stah/	journalist m/f
la giornalista	lah jyohr·nah·lee·stah	
giovedì	jyoh·veh·dee	Thursday
giugno	jyoo·nyoh	June
la gonna	lah goh·nah	skirt
grasso/grassa	grah·soh/grah·sah	fat m/f
i guanti	ee gwahn·tee	gloves

I

ieri	yeh·ree	yesterday adv
ieri sera	yeh·ree say·rah	last night adv
l'impiegato/	leem·pyeh·gah·toh/	employee m/f
l'impiegata	leem·pyeh·gah·tah	
l'indirizzo	leen·dee·ree·tsoh	address
l'iniezione	lee·nyeh·tsyoh·neh	injection, shot
inglese	een·glay·say	English
l'insalata	leen·sah·lah·tah	salad
l'inverno	leen·vehr·noh	winter

Irlanda	eer·lahn·dah	Ireland
irlandese	eer·lahn·deh·seh	Irish
Italia	ee·tah·lyah	Italy
italiano/	ee·tah·lyah·noy/	Italian m/f
italiana	ee·tah·lyah·nah	

L

la L	lah eh·leh	large (size)
il latte	eel lah·teh	milk
il lavoro	eel lah·voy·roh	work n
la lezione	lah leh·tsyoh·neh	class
lontano	lohn·tah·noh	far
luglio	loo·lly·oh	July
lunedì	loo·neh·dee	Monday
i luoghi	ee lwoh·ghee	places

M

la M	lah eh·meh	medium (size)
la macchina	lah mah·kee·nah	car
la madre	lah mah·dreh	mother
maggio	mah·jyoh	May
la maglietta	lah mah·llyeh·tah	T-shirt
il maglione	eel mah·llyoh·neh	sweater
magro/magra	mah·groh/mah·grah	slender m/f
il mal di denti	eel mahl dee dehn·tee	toothache
il mal di gola	eel mahl dee goh·lah	sore throat
il mal di pancia	eel mahl dee pahn·chyah	stomachache
il mal di testa	eel mahl dee teh·stah	headache
malato/malata	mah·lah·toh/mah·lah·tah	sick m/f
mangiare	mahn·jyah·reh	eat v
il marito	eel mah·ree·toh	husband
martedì	mahr·teh·dee	Tuesday
marzo	mahr·tsoh	March
la medicina	lah meh·dee·chee·nah	medicine
mercoledì	mehr·koh·leh·dee	Wednesday
il mese	eel may·seh	month

mesi dell'anno	ee may·see dehl·ah·noh	months of the year
mezzanotte	meh·dzah·noh·teh	midnight
mezzo	meh·dzoh	half
mezzogiorno	meh·dzoh·jyohr·noh	noon
il minuto	eel mee·noo·toh	minute
la moglie	lah moh·llyeh	wife
il monumento	eel moh·noo·mehn·toh	monument

N

nero/nera	nay·roh/nay·rah	black m/f
la neve	lah nay·veh	snow n
il nipote	eel nee·poh·teh	nephew/grandson
la nipote	lah nee·poh·teh	niece/granddaughter
la nonna	lah noh·nah	grandmother
il nonno	eel noh·noh	grandfather
notte	noh·teh	night
novembre	noh·vehm·breh	November
nubile	noo·bee·leh	single f
il numero	eel noo·meh·roh	number
numeroso/	noo·meh·roy·soh/	big m/f
numerosa	noo·meh·roy·sah	
nuvoloso/	noo·voh·loy·soh/	cloudy m/f
nuvolosa	noo·voh·loy·sah	
il nuoto	eel nwoh·toh	swimming

O

oggi	oh·jee	today
l'ora	loy·rah	hour
l'ospedale	loh·speh·dah·leh	hospital
otto	oh·toh	8
ottobre	oh·toh·breh	October

adj	adjective	adv	adverb	BE	British English	n	noun	v verb

P

il padre	eel pah·dreh	father
la palestra	lah pah·leh·strah	gym
la pallacanestro	lah pah·lah·kah·neh·stroh	basketball
la pallavolo	lah pah·lah·voy·loh	volleyball
il pane	eel pah·neh	bread
i pantaloncini	ee pahn·tah·lohn·chee·nee	shorts
i pantaloni	ee pahn·tah·loh·nee	pants, trousers
il passaporto	eel pah·sah·pohr·toh	passport
le patate	leh pah·tah·teh	potatoes
la pasta	lah pah·stah	pasta
le persone	leh pehr·soh·neh	people
pesare	pay·sah·reh	weigh v
il pesce	eel pay·sheh	fish
il peso	eel pay·soh	weight
il pollo	eel poy·loh	chicken
la posizione	lah poh·see·tsyoh·neh	location
la posta	lah poh·stah	mail n, post office
prendere	prehn·deh·reh	take, eat, drink v
presto	preh·stoh	early adv
la primavera	lah pree·mah·veh·rah	spring
la professione	lah proh·feh·syoh·neh	job, profession
il professore	eel proh·feh·soh·reh	teacher, professor m
la professoressa	lah proh·feh·soh·ray·sah	teacher, professor f
in punto	een poon·toh	o'clock

Q

quaranta	kwah·rahn·tah	40
un quarto	oon kwahr·toh	quarter
quattordici	kwah·tohr·dee·chee	14
quattro	kwah·troh	4
quindici	kween·dee·chee	15

R

il raffreddore	eel rah·freh·doy·reh	cold n
Regno Unito	ray·nyoh oo·nee·toh	United Kingdom (U.K.)
la ricetta	lah ree·cheh·tah	prescription
la rivista	lah ree·vee·stah	magazine
il riso	eel ree·soh	rice
rosa	roh·zah	pink
rosso/rossa	roy·soh/roy·sah	red m/f

S

la S	lah eh·seh	small (size)
sabato	sah·bah·toh	Saturday
la sala da pranzo	lah sah·lah dah prahn·tsoh	dining room
la salute	lah sah·loo·teh	health
sano/sana	sah·noh/sah·nah	healthy m/f
la sciarpa	lah shyahr·pah	scarf
lo scontrino	loh skohn·tree·noh	receipt
la scuola	lah skwoh·lah	school
il secondo	eel seh·kohn·doh	second
sedici	seh·dee·chee	16
il segretario/ la segretaria	eel seh·greh·tah·ryoh/ lah seh·greh·tah·ryah	secretary m/f
sessanta	seh·sahn·tah	60
sei	say	6
la sera	lah say·rah	evening
sette	seh·teh	7
settembre	seh·tehm·breh	September
la settimana scorsa	lah seh·tee·mah·nah scoyr·sah	last week adv
a sinistra	ah see·nee·strah	to the left
il soggiorno	eel soh·jyohr·noh	living room
i soldi	ee sohl·dee	money
il sole	eel soy·leh	sun

adj	adjective	adv	adverb	BE	British English	n noun	v verb

la sorella	lah soh·reh·lah	sister
gli sport	lly spohrt	sports
sposato/	spoh·zah·toh/	married m/f
sposata	spoh·zah·tah	
le stagioni	leh stah·jyoh·nee	seasons
la stanza	lah stahn·tsah	room
la stazione	lah stah·tsyoh·neh	train station
ferroviaria	feh·roh·vyah·ryah	
Stati Uniti	stah·tee oo·nee·tee	United States
la stazione della	lah stah·tsyoh·neh deh·lah	subway station
metropolitana	meh·troh·poh·lee·tah·nah	
lo stipendio	loh stee·pehn·dyoh	salary
la strada	lah strah·dah	street
stressato/	streh·sah·toh/	stressed m/f
stressata	streh·sah·tah	
il succo	eel soo·koh	juice n
il supermercato	eel soo·pehr·mehr·kah·toh	supermarket
Svizzera	svee·tsay·rah	Switzerland
svizzero/	svee·tsay·roy/	Swiss m/f
svizzera	svee·tsay·rah	

trenta	trayn·tah	30
trentadue	trayn·tah·dweh	32
trentacinque	trayn·tah·cheen·kweh	35
trentanove	trayn·tah·noh·veh	39
trentasei	trayn·tah·say	36
trentasette	trayn·tah·seh·teh	37
trentatré	trayn·tah·tray	33
trentotto	trayn·toh·toh	38
trentuno	trayn·too·noh	31

U

l'uccello	loo·cheh·loy	bird
l'ufficio	loo·fee·chyoh	office
l'ufficio postale	loo·fee·chyoh poh·stah·leh	post office
umido/umida	oo·mee·doh/oo·mee·dah	humid m/f
undici	oon·dee·chee	11
unito/unita	oo·nee·toh/oo·nee·tah	close m/f
l'uomo	lwoh·moy	man
l'uovo	lwoh·voh	egg

T

tardi	tahr·dee	late adv
il tè	eel teh	tea
il telefono	eel teh·leh·foh·noh	telephone
il teatro	eel teh·ah·troh	theater, theatre BE
il tempo	eel tehm·poh	weather
il tennis	eel teh·nees	tennis
la torta	lah toyr·tah	cake
la tosse	lah toy·seh	cough n
tra	trah	between
tre	tray	3
tredici	tray·dee·chee	13

V

la vacanza	lah vah·kahn·tsah	vacation, holiday BE
la valigia	lah vah·lee·jyah	suitcase
venerdì	veh·nehr·dee	Friday
venti	vayn·tee	20
il vento	eel vehn·toh	wind
verde	vayr·deh	green
viola	vyoh·lah	purple
volere bene	voh·leh·reh beh·neh	to love
il volo	eel voy·loh	flight
il volo diretto	eel voy·loh dee·reh·toh	nonstop flight

adj	adjective	adv	adverb	BE	British English	n	noun	v verb

Numbers

i numeri	ee noo·meh·ree	numbers
zero	dzeh·roh	0
uno	oo·noh	1
due	dweh	2
tre	tray	3
quattro	kwah·troh	4
cinque	cheen·kweh	5
sei	say	6
sette	seh·teh	7
otto	oh·toh	8
nove	noh·veh	9
dieci	dyeh·chee	10
undici	oon·dee·chee	11
dodici	doh·dee·chee	12
tredici	tray·dee·chee	13
quattordici	kwah·tohr·dee·chee	14
quindici	kween·dee·chee	15
sedici	seh·dee·chee	16
diciassette	dyah·chyah·seh·teh	17
diciotto	dee·chyoh·toh	18
diciannove	dee·chyah·noh·veh	19
venti	vayn·tee	20
trenta	trayn·tah	30
trentuno	trayn·too·noh	31
trentadue	trayn·tah·dweh	32
trentatré	trayn·tah·tray	33
trentaquattro	trayn·tah·kwah·troh	34
trentacinque	trayn·tah·cheen·kweh	35
trentasei	trayn·tah·say	36
trentasette	trayn·tah·seh·teh	37
trentotto	trayn·toh·toh	38
trentanove	trayn·tah·noh·veh	39
quaranta	wah·rahn·tah	40
cinquanta	cheen·kwahn·tah	50
sessanta	seh·sahn·tah	60

Days

i giorni	ee jyohr·nee	days
lunedì	loo·neh·dee	Monday
martedì	mahr·teh·dee	Tuesday
mercoledì	mehr·koh·leh·dee	Wednesday
giovedì	jyoh·veh·dee	Thursday
venerdì	veh·nehr·dee	Friday
sabato	sah·bah·toh	Saturday
domenica	doh·meh·nee·kah	Sunday

Months

i mesi	may·see	months
gennaio	jeh·nah·yoh	January
febbraio	feh·brah·yoh	February
marzo	mahr·tsoh	March
aprile	ah·pree·leh	April
maggio	mah·jyoh	May
giugno	jyoo·nyoh	June
luglio	loo·lly·oh	July
agosto	ah·goh·stoh	August
settembre	eh·tehm·breh	September
ottobre	oh·toh·breh	October
novembre	noh·vehm·breh	November
dicembre	dee·chehm·breh	December

adj adjective   adv adverb   BE British English   n noun   v verb

Colors

i colori   ee koh·<u>loh</u>·ree   colors, colours BE

giallo/gialla
<u>jyah</u>·loh/<u>jyah</u>·lah
yellow m/f

nero/nera
<u>nay</u>·roh/<u>nay</u>·rah
black m/f

blu
bloo
blue

rosso/rossa
<u>roy</u>·soh/<u>roy</u>·sah
red m/f

bianco/bianca
<u>byahn</u>·koh/<u>byahn</u>·kah
white m/f

rosa
<u>roh</u>·zah
pink

viola
<u>vyoh</u>·lah
purple

verde
<u>vayr</u>·deh
green

Seasons

l'inverno

leen·<u>vehr</u>·noh

winter

la primavera

lah pree·mah·<u>veh</u>·rah

spring

l'estate

leh·<u>stah</u>·teh

summer

l'autunno

low·<u>too</u>·noh

autumn, fall

---

adj   adjective   adv   adverb   BE   British English   n   noun   v   verb

Countries/Nationalities

| Canada | kah·nah·dah | Canada |
| canadese | kah·nah·deh·seh | Canadian |

| Irlanda | eer·lahn·dah | Ireland |
| irlandese | eer·lahn·deh·seh | Irish |

Italia	ee·tah·yah	Italy
italiano	ee·tah·yah·noh	Italian m
italiana	ee·tah·yah·nah	Italian f

| Regno Unito | ray·nyoh oo·nee·toh | United Kingdom |
| inglese | een·glay·say | English |

Stati Uniti	stah·tee oo·nee·tee	United States
americano	ah·may·ree·kah·noh	American m
americana	ah·may·ree·kah·nah	American f

Svizzera	svee·tsay·rah	Switzerland
svizzero	svee·tsay·roy	Swiss m
svizzera	svee·tsay·rah	Swiss f

| adj | adjective | adv | adverb | BE | British English | n | noun | v | verb |

Extra Words

Italian	Pronunciation	English
anch'io	ahn·kyoh	likewise
ancora	ahn·koy·rah	still adv
gli affari	lly ah·fah·ree	business
l'albergo	lahl·behr·goh	hotel
l'articolo	lahr·tee·koh·loh	article
assunto/assunta	ah·soon·toh/ah·soon·tah	hired m/f
l'azienda	lah·dzyehn·dah	company
il cambio	eel kahm·byoh	change (money)
i centesimi	ee chehn·teh·zee·mee	cents
la cognata	lah koh·nyah·tah	sister-in-law
il cognato	eel koh·nyah·toh	brother-in-law
correre	koh·reh·reh	run v
il datore	eel dah·toy·reh	employer
di lavoro	dee lah·voy·roh	
difficile	dee·fee·chee·leh	difficult
la dogana	lah doh·gah·nah	customs
facile	fah·chee·leh	easy
la finestra	lah fee·neh·strah	window
francese	frahn·cheay·say	French
il genero	eel jeh·neh·roh	son-in-law
il giardino	eel jyahr·dee·noh	garden
giocare	jyoh·kah·reh	play v
indossare	een·doh·sah·reh	wear v
l'isolato	ee·zoh·lah·toh	block
il maggiore	eel mah·jyoh·reh	oldest
il minore	eel mee·noh·reh	youngest
molto	moyl·toh	a lot
la nuora	lah nwoh·rah	daughter-in-law
nuotare	nwoh·tah·reh	swim v
il pavimento	eel pah·vee·mayn·toh	floor
Piacere	pyah·cheh·reh	Nice to meet you
la piazza	lah pyah·tsah	square
il portafoglio	eel pohr·tah·foh·llyoh	wallet
portare	pohr·tah·reh	wear v
portoghese	poyr·toy·ghay·say	Portuguese
la prenotazione	lah preh·noh·tah·tsyoh·neh	reservation
il resto	eel reh·stoh	change
le scale	leh skah·leh	stairs
lo scalo	loh skah·loh	stopover
le scarpe	leh skahr·peh	shoes
gli spiccioli	lly spee·chyoh·lee	small change
la suocera	lah swoh·cheh·rah	mother-in-law
il suocero	eel swoh·cheh·roh	father-in-law
tedesco/tedesca	tay·day·skoy/tay·day·skah	German m/f
viaggiare	vyah·jyah·reh	travel v

adj	adjective	adv	adverb	BE	British English

n   noun   v   verb

Unit 1 Lesson 1

Activity A

1 T; 2 T; 3 F; 4 F

Activity B

Mi chiamo Lisa. **Come si chiama?**; Mi chiamo Marco. **Piacere.**; Sono italiana. E Lei, **di dov'è?**; Sono svizzero.

Lesson 2

Activity A

1 Ciao!; 2 Come si chiama?; 3 Di dov'è?; 4 Ciao!/ Arrivederci.

Activity B

1 Buona sera.; 2 Buona notte.; 3 Buon giorno.

Lesson 3

Activity A

America del Nord, top to bottom: 6; 4; Europa, top to bottom: 2; 3; 1; 5

Activity B

From left to right: 4; 3; 1; 2

Lesson 4

Activity A

1 io; 2 lei; 3 lui; 4 tu

Activity B

1 voi; 2 loro; 3 noi

Activity C

1 io; 2 lei; 3 lui; 4 noi; 5 loro

Lesson 5

Activity A

lingua; nazionalità; italiano; inglese

Activity B

1 a; 2 b; 3 b; 4 b

Lesson 6

Activity A

1 svizzera; 2 americana; 3 inglese; 4 australiano

Activity B

1 italiana; 2 inglese; 3 svizzera; 4 americana; 5 canadese

Lesson 7

Activity A

1 È italiano?; 2 Parlo bene.; 3 Un po'.

Your Turn

Answers may vary. Possible answers:
Q1 Buon giorno! Mi chiamo Massimo. Come si chiama?
A1 Sono Adriano, piacere.
Q2 Di dov'è?
A2 Sono italiano.

Lesson 8

Activity A

1 sono; 2 è; 3 sei; 4 è

Activity B

1 siete; 2 siamo; 3 sono

Your Turn

è; sono; siete; Sono; è

Review

Activity A

Nome	Paese	Nazionalità
Laura	Italia	italiana
Massimo	Svizzera	svizzera
Cassandra	Canada	canadese
Brian	Stati Uniti	americano
Katie	Regno Unito	inglese

Activity B

1 Tu sei americano.; Lisa è italiana.; Lei è canadese.; Adriano è italiano.

Activity C

Guida Buon giorno! Benvenuto in Italia!
Kiko Buon giorno! Sono Kiko Buxó. Kiko Buxó. **Come si chiama?**
Guida Mi chiamo Enrico. Piacere.
Kiko Piacere. È italiano?
Guida Sì. Di dov'è?
Kiko Sono inglese. Parla inglese?
Guida Un po'.
Kiko Parlo inglese e spagnolo.
Guida Bene!
Kiko Arrivederci, Enrico.
Guida Arrivederci!

Activity D

Challenge

Croazia

Activity E

1 Buon giorno! Mi chiamo Laura.; 2 Noi siamo canadesi.; 3 Io sono italiano.; 4 Manuel è americano.; 5 Io parlo inglese.; 6 Anna è italiana.

Unit 2 Lesson 1

Activity A   1 F; 2 F; 3 T; 4 T

Activity B

1 persone: bambini; bambine; uomini; donne
2 cose: case; edifici; macchine; autobus
3 animali: gatti; cani

Lesson 2

Activity A

1 a uccello; b donna; c uomo; d bambino
2 a uomo; b autobus; c cane; d bambino; e edificio; f gatto; g donna; h macchina

Activity B

1 maschile; 2 maschile; 3 femminile; 4 femminile; 5 maschile; 6 femminile; maschile; maschile

Lesson 3

Activity A   1 Guarda le persone! 2 Guarda gli animali!

Activity B

Cara Elena,
I'm having a great time here, and I'm learning some italiano.
Guarda le persone! There are uomini, donne e bambini.
Guarda le case! Guarda l'edificio! Guarda gli animali! There are cani, gatti e uccelli.
Mi manchi.

Lesson 4

Activity A   1 bambini; 2 borse; 3 matite; tori

Activity B   1 il; 2 la; 3 i; 4 le; 5 la; 6 l'

Activity C   1 il gatto; 2 le donne; 3 le macchine; 4 la casa

Your Turn   1 le; 2 gli; 3 l'; 4 lo/gli; 5 il

Lesson 5

Activity A   1 c; 2 d; 3 b; 4 a

Activity B

Via: Verdi; Numero 12;
Città: Firenze; Stato: Italia

Lesson 6

Activity A

diciannove,
ventiquattro, venticinque, ventisei, ventisette, ventotto, ventinove

Activity B

1 uno	4 quattro
6 sei	9 nove
13 tredici	12 dodici
18 diciotto	15 quindici
10 dieci	22 ventidue
30 trenta	14 quattordici

Activity C

1 14 Verdi Street; 27 Leopardi Avenue;
3 Telephone: (02) 221-410; 4 Zip Code: 97019

Lesson 7

Activity A

Answers may vary. Possible answers:
Mi chiamo_____.; Il mio compleanno è _____.;
Il mio indirizzo è _____.; Il mio numero di telefono è_____.

Activity B   1 a; 2 a; 3 a; 4 b

Lesson 8

Activity A

io parlo; tu parli; lui/lei parla; noi parliamo; voi parlate; loro parlano

Activity B

io vivo; tu vivi; Lei/lui/lei vive; noi viviamo; voi vivete; loro vivono

Activity C

Tom vive in Via Orchard 10; Julia e Max vivono in Via Providence 24; Io e Laura viviamo in Via Main 16

Your Turn   Io insegno inglese e italiano; Laura insegna inglese.

Review

Activity A

1 tre bambini; 2 una casa; 3 due gatti; cinque donne

Activity B

1 Andrea vive in Viale 4, numero 8. ; 2 Il numero di telefono di Tom è quarantotto, ventinove, tredici, settantatré, novantuno.; 3 Corinne e Mark vivono in Via 4, numero 30.; Il numero di telefono di Laura è quarantaquattro, ottantadue, ottantadue, ventisette, diciannove, ottantaquattro.; Tom vive in Via Huron, numero 25.

Activity C

1 gli; 2 le; 3 l'/gli; lo

Challenge

Answers may vary. Possible answers:
Lei cammina in Via verdi.; Loro camminano in Via Verdi.; Lui legge molto.; Loro leggono molto.

Activity D

Laura Buon giorno. Come si chiama?
Lei   Buon giorno. Mi chiamo (your name).
Laura Bene. Qual è il suo numero di telefono?
Lei   Il mio numero di telefono è (your phone number).
Laura Qual è il suo indirizzo?
Lei   Il mio indirizzo è (your address).
Laura E il codice di avviamento postale?
Lei   Il mio codice di avviamento postale è (your zip code).
Laura Infine, qual è la sua data di nascita?
Lei   La mia data di nascita è (your date of birth).
Laura Benissimo! Benvenuto all'Istituto di Lingue Dante Alighieri.
Lei   Molte grazie.

Unit 3 Lesson 1

Activity A

1 Sono le diciotto e trentacinque; 2 Mancano cinquantacinque minuti; 3 Novanta minuti; 4 La Roma

Activity B

1 Che ore sono?; 2 Sono le diciotto e trentacinque; 3 È presto! Quanto tempo manca alla fine della partita?; 4 Mancano cinquantacinque minuti.

Lesson 2

Activity A

1 Sono le tre e quarantacinque; 2 È l'una e un quarto; 3 Sono le otto e trenta; 4 Sono le dodici or È mezzogiorno/mezzanotte.

Activity B

1 È presto!; 2 È tardi!; 3 È presto!; 4 È tardi!

Activity C

1 Che ore sono?; 2 È presto!; 3 È tardi!; 4 Sono le due.

Lesson 3

Activity A

1 quarantaquattro; 2 trentadue; 3 sessantasette; 4 cinquantotto

Activity B

1 Mancano quindici minuti.; 2 Manca un'ora e quindici minuti.; 3 Manca un'ora e quarantacinque minuti.; 4 Manca un minuto.

Your Turn

Sono le sedici e dodici. Mancano trentatré minuti.; Sono le quattro e ventidue. Mancano ventitré minuti.; Sono le quattro e trentadue. Mancano tredici minuti.; Sono le quattro e quaranta-due. Mancano tre minuti.

Lesson 4

Activity A

io	parto
tu	parti
Lei	parte
lui/lei	parte
noi	partiamo
voi	partite
loro	partono

Activity B

1 Io offro; 2 Lei apre; Lui pulisce; 4 Io costruisco

Lesson 5

Activity A

1 a ; 2 a; 3 b; 4 a; 5 b

Activity B

1 fare i compiti; 2 fare una telefonata; 3 fare la lavatrice; 4 fare ginnastica

Lesson 6

Activity A

1 martedì; 2 lunedì e giovedì; 3 venerdì; 4 mercoledì e sabato; 5 domenica

Activity B

1 lunedì, 17 novembre; 2 sabato, 5 giugno; 3 mercoledì 21 settembre; 4 venerdì 8 aprile; 5 martedì 31 gennaio; 6 domenica 12 agosto; 7 giovedì 25 marzo; 8 domenica 14 ottobre; 9 lunedì 29 maggio; 10 martedì 2 dicembre; 11 venerdì 15 luglio; 12 mercoledì 18 febbraio

Lesson 7

Activity A

1 b; 2 b; 3 a; 4 b

Activity B

1 Che giorno è oggi?; 2 Quanti ne abbiamo oggi?; 3 In che mese siamo?; 4 In che anno siamo?

Lesson 8

Activity A

1 fai; 2 fa; 3 facciamo; 4 fate

Activity B

1 c; 2 a; 3 b; 4 d; 5 e

Your Turn

Answers will vary but make sure to include *faccio* in the answer; possible answers may be:
Faccio la spesa il sabato.
Faccio ginnastica la domenica.

Review

Activity A

Activities may be in a different order than what you wrote.
2 Irene fa la spesa alle dieci.; 3 Irene fa la lavatrice alle diciotto; 4 Irene fa ginnastica alle sedici; 5 Irene fa i compiti alle ventuno e trenta.

Activity B

1 Mancano due ore, trentaquattro minuti e tredici secondi.; 2 Mancano ventisette secondi.; 3 Mancano dodici minuti e trentanove secondi.

Activity C

1 sabato, tredici febbraio; 2 lunedì, quindici febbraio; 3 martedì, ventitré febbraio; 4 domenica, ventuno febbraio

Unit 4 Lesson 1

Activity A

1 F; 2 T; 3 F; 4 F

Activity B

1 a; 2 a; 3 b; 4 b; 5 b

Lesson 2

Activity A

Siamo in cinque nella mia **famiglia**. Tommaso è mio **padre**. Mia **madre** si chiama Marina. Giulia è mia **sorella**. Marco è il **marito** di Giulia.

Activity B

1 fratelli; 2 fratello; 3 madre; 4 padre; 5 genitori; 6 figlio; 7 figlia; 8 figli; 9 moglie; 10 marito

Lesson 3

Activity A

1 È numerosa la sua famiglia?; 2 Nella mia famiglia siamo in otto. Guardi questa foto.; 3 Che famiglia numerosa!; 4 Sì, la mia famiglia è numerosa. E la sua famiglia è numerosa?; 5 No. La mia famiglia è poco numerosa. Siamo in quattro.

Activity B

1 Che famiglia poco numerosa!; 2 Che famiglia numerosa!; 3 Che famiglia numerosa!; 4 Che famiglia poco numerosa!

Lesson 4

Activity A

1 mia; 2 la tua; 3 La sua; 4 le mie; 5 i tuoi; 6 i suoi; 7 La nostra; 8 i nostri

Activity B

1 e; 2 b; 3 h; 4 d; 5 c; 6 g; 7 a; 8 f

Lesson 5

Activity A

1 suo nonno; 2 sua madre; 3 sua cugina; 4 sua nipote

Activity B

1 il cugino; 2 la cugina; 3 la nonna; 4 il nipote

Lesson 6

Activity A

1 cugina; 2 nipote; 3 zia; 4 nuora; 5 nonno; 6 nonni

Activity B

1 a; 2 a; 3 b; 4 a; 5 a; 6 b

Lesson 7

Activity A

1 Sì, la mia famiglia è molto unita.; 2 No, è celibe.; 3 Sì, ho una famiglia numerosa.; 4 No, sono sposata. Quello è mio marito.

Activity B

1 Ti amo.; 2 Ti voglio bene.; 3 Ho una famiglia unita.; 4 È sposato/sposata?

Lesson 8

Activity A

1 un nonno or un uomo; 2 una macchina; 3 un'amica or una ragazza; 4 uno zoo

Activity B

Answers will vary. **Possible answers: 1 Tu hai un fratello.; 2 Io ho un cugino.; 3 Loro hanno una zia.; 4 Voi avete un/una nipote.**

Your Turn

Answers will vary. 1 Sì, ho due zii/ No, non ho zii.; 2 Sì, Ho tre nipoti/ No, non ho nipoti.; 3 Sì, i miei zii hanno due figli/ No, i miei zii non hanno figli.; 4 Sì, i miei cugini hanno un figlio/ No, i miei cugini non hanno figli.

Review

Activity A

Serena	Questo è mio **nonno**, Alfonso. E questa è mia **nonna**, Giulia.
Carlo	Chi è questa signora?
Serena	Lei è mia **cugina**, Laura, e questo è suo **fratello**, Giuseppe.
Carlo	È tua **madre** quella signora?
Serena	No, quella è mia **zia**, Sara. Laura e Giuseppe sono i suoi **figli**.
Carlo	È questa tua **madre**?
Serena	No, questa è mia **zia** Linda, la **moglie** di mio **zio** Giovanni. Lui è il **fratello** di mio **padre**.
Carlo	La tua **famiglia** è numerosa. E dov'è tua **madre**?
Serena	I miei **genitori** non sono alla festa.

Activity B

1 Giulia è sua nonna; 2 Laura e Giuseppe sono i suoi cugini; 3 Sara e Linda sono le sue zie; 4 Giovanni è suo zio.

Activity C

Answers will vary. Possible answers:

Carlo	La mia famiglia è numerosa/ La mia famiglia è poco numerosa.
Carlo	Sì, ho un fratello/ No, non ho fratelli.
Carlo	Sì, ho molti zii/ No, non ho zii.

Activity D

Carlo	**Quel** bambino è suo nipote?
Alfonso	No, **questo** bambino è mio nipote.
Carlo	**Quella** signora è sua moglie?
Alfonso	No, **questa** signora è mia moglie.
Carlo	**Quelle** ragazze sono le sue figlie?
Alfonso	No, **queste** ragazze sono le mie figlie.

Activity E

1 Loro hanno due figli.; 2 Loro hanno tre figli.; 3 Lei ha due figli.; 4 Lui ha un figlio.

Answer Key

Unit 5 Lesson 1

Activity A 1 T; 2 T; 3 F; 4 F

Activity B 1 a; 2 b; 3 b; 4 b

Lesson 2

Activity A 1 la frutta; 2 il caffè; 3 la zuppa; 4 la birra

Activity B 1 Mangio del pane e bevo del caffè.; 2 Mangio della pasta e bevo dell'acqua.; 3 Mangio della frutta e bevo del vino.

Lesson 3

Activity A 1 Ho fame.; 2 Ho sete.; 3 Ho fame.; 4 Ho sete.; 5 Ho fame.; 6 Ho sete.

Activity B 1 Ho voglia di mangiare.; 2 Ho voglia di bere.

Activity C 1 Facciamo colazione!; 2 Pranziamo!; 3 Ceniamo!

Lesson 4

Activity A 1 Dove; 2 Qual; 3 Che cosa; 4 Quando.

Activity B Possible answers: 1 Quali sono i suoi fratelli?; 2 Come mai non va al cinema?; 3 Perché è triste?; 4 Chi sono quelle persone?; 5 Quanti anni ha?

Activity C 1 Perché; 2 Chi; 3 Quando; 4 Quale; 5 Dove

Your Turn 1 Come si chiama sua madre?; 2 Dove abita?; 3 Chi sono quelli?; 4 Che ore sono?

Lesson 5

Activity A 1 b; 2 a; 3 b; 4 a

Activity B 1 Buon giorno, che cosa desidera?; 2 Vorrei un secondo.; 3 Vuole anche un contorno?; 4 Sì, prendo l'insalata mista.

Lesson 6

Activity A 1 primo; 2 secondo; 3 dolce; 4 contorno; 5 antipasto

Activity B 1 Un antipasto è la bruschetta (a); 2 Un secondo piatto è la bistecca (b); 3 Un dolce è la torta al cioccolato (a)

Your Turn
Answers may vary.
Possible answers are:

Ristorante _____
Menu
Antipasti
Bruschetta
Primi piatti
Spaghetti al pomodoro
Secondi piatti
Pollo arrosto
Contorni
Insalata mista
Dolci
Gelato
Bevande
Acqua
Vino

Lesson 7

Activity A 1 Buon appetito.; 2 Il conto, per favore.; 3 È molto buono.; 4 Posso vedere la carta dei vini?

Activity B 1 b; 2 a; 3 b; 4 a

Your Turn Answers may vary.

Lesson 8

Activity A 1 vuole; 2 vogliamo; 3 vogliono; 4 vuoi

Activity B
1 Voglio il pollo; 2 Non voglio il formaggio; 3 Voglio il pesce; 4 Non voglio la pasta; 5 Voglio la torta; 6 Non voglio le verdure.

Review

Activity A

A pranzo (volere)
1 Voglio; 2 Vuoi; 3 Vuole; 4 Vogliamo; 5 Volete; 6 Vogliono
A cena (preferire)
1 Preferisco; 2 Preferisci; 3 Preferisce; 4 Preferiamo; 5 Preferite; 6 Preferiscono

Activity B

Trattoria Italia
Menu
Antipasti
Bruschetta
Primi
Risotto ai funghi
Secondi
Pollo arrosto
Pesce alla griglia
Dolci
Tiramisù
Torta al cioccolato

Activity C
Mario Ho fame.
Lucia Che cosa vuoi mangiare?
Mario Vorrei del pesce.
Lucia Andiamo a cena.

In the car
Mario Dov'è il ristorante?
Lucia È là.

At the restaurant before eating
Lucia Che vuoi come primo?
Mario Vorrei la pasta.

At the restaurant after eating
Lucia Cameriere, il conto, per favore.

120 **Berlitz** 5-Minute Italian

Unit 6 Lesson 1

Activity A

1 c; 2 d; 3 b; 4 a

Activity B

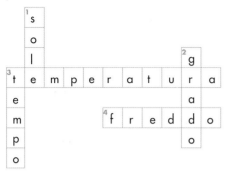

Crossword:
- 1 (down) s o l temperatura (tempo down)
- 2 (down) g r a d o
- 3 (across) t e m p e r a t u r a
- 4 (across) f r e d d o

Lesson 2

Activity A

Che tempo fa in Svizzera?; Fa freddo e è nuvoloso.; Qual è la temperatura?; Ci sono dieci gradi.; Davvero? Qui fa caldo. È umido.

Activity B

1 a ; 2 b; 3 b; 4 b

Activity C

1 c; 2 b; 3 a; 4 d

Lesson 3

Activity A

Qual è la temperatura?	Che tempo fa?
35°C	Fa caldo.
6°C	Fa bel tempo.
32°F	Fa freddo.

Activity B   1 b; 2 d; 3 a; 4 c

Activity C   1 a; 2 a; 3 b

Lesson 4

Activity A

1 la bella ragazza; 2 il piccolo cane; 3 la macchina rossa; 4 il ragazzo americano; 5 la tavola rotonda

Activity B

1 a; 2 a; 3 b; 4 b

Your Turn   Answers will vary.

Lesson 5

Activity A

attività in estate: giocare a calcio; nuotare; correre
vestiti in inverno: cappotto; guanti; sciarpa

Activity B   1 plays soccer; 2 winter; 3 winter; 4 Italy, 33

Lesson 6

Activity A   Answers will vary between è divertente and è noioso.

Activity B   1 Che sta facendo?; 2 Che fa di solito?; 3 Durante l'inverno di solito (viaggio, etc).4 Ha ragione.

Your Turn   Answers may vary. Possible answers are:

Andare al mare è divertente.; 2 Fare le pulizie è noioso.; 3 Giocare a calcio è divertente.; 4 Fare ginnastica è noioso.

Lesson 7

Activity A   1 i guanti; 2 il cappotto; 3 la maglietta

Activity B   1 l'autunno; 2 la primavera; 3 l'inverno; 4 l'estate

Activity C   1 giacca; 2 guanti; 3 maglietta; 4 pantaloncini

Lesson 8

Activity A   1 Io sto viaggiando, tu stai viaggiando, Lei, lui/lei sta viaggiando, noi stiamo viaggiando, voi state viaggiando, loro stanno viaggiando

Activity B   1 Io sto viaggiando.; 2 Lui sta giocando.; 3 Loro stanno correndo.; 4 Tu stai nuotando.

Activity C   1 Maria gioca a calcio.; 2 Noi giochiamo a calcio.; 3 Io gioco a calcio.; 4 Tu giochi a calcio.

Activity D   1 Gioco a pallavolo.; 2 Gioco a golf.; 3 Gioco a carte.; 4 Gioco a calcio.

Review

Activity A   1 Io sto studiando.; 2 Lui sta correndo.; 3 Noi stiamo partendo.; 4 Sta piovendo.; 5 Lei sta nuotando.

Activity B   1 La macchina blu.; 2 Una bella casa.; 3 Un giovane ragazzo.; 4 Un uomo italiano.; 5 Un cappotto caro.

Activity C

```
B P E V Z L Z S C S H N W Y J
X C L A C H A Q U E T E W V V
Q P Y C X Q Z M K D Y V P Y C
E D S L A P R I M A V E R A E
R D O B M N A B R Z E K P E S
R E L F L M S V L E A D O I T
E A E A T E M P E R A T U R A
V Q Z Z Z Q G A L Q N W P E H T
O Z Z Z Q G A L Q N W P E H T
I E S T A C A L I D T D L L E
P I J U G A R C A L D O J K W
B K V F Z R H V R E P J U O D
S Q W R J P K A P P J R N Y U
I T O D D E R F D B X L Q X N
```

Activity D

1 Sta nevicando.; 2 Fa freddo.; 3 C'è vento.

Challenge

Gioco a calcio quando sta piovendo.

Unit 7 Lesson 1

Activity A

1 c; 2 b; 3 b

Activity B

1a; 2 b; 3 a

Lesson 2

Activity A

1 a; 2 a; 3 b; 4 a

Activity B

1 Sto cercando un vestito.; 2 Porto la (taglia) M.; 3 Vorrei comprare una gonna.; 4 Porto la S.

Lesson 3

Activity A

1 il maglione; 2 i pantaloni; 3 il vestito; 4 la camicia; la gonna

Activity B

1 a; 2 a; 3 a; 4 a

Lesson 4

Activity A

1 si; 2 ci; 3 si; 4 ti

Activity B

1 vestono; 2 vesti; 3 vesto; 4 veste; 5 vestiamo

Your Turn

alzo	lavo	sveglio	metto
alzi	lavi	svegli	metti
alza	lava	sveglia	mette
alza	lava	sveglia	mette
alziamo	laviamo	svegliamo	mettiamo
alzate	lavate	svegliate	mettete
alzano	lavano	svegliano	mettono

Lesson 5

Activity A

1 b; 2 a; 3 a; 4 b

Activity B

1 b; 2 b; 3 a; 4 a

Lesson 6

Activity A

1 Accetta il bancomat?; 2 Quanto costa la gonna?; 3 Accetta assegni?; 4 Vorrei pagare con la carta di credito; 5 Quanto costano i pantaloni?

Activity B

1 care; 2 cara; 3 poco; 4 molto

Lesson 7

Activity A

1 assegno; 2 il bancomat; 3 lo scontrino; 4 soldi

Activity B

Ho 500 **euro** in **contanti** nel mio portafoglio. Ho anche una **carta di credito**. Voglio comprare molti vestiti perché il **cambio** è favorevole.

Lesson 8

Activity A

1 più della; 2 più del; 3 meno del; 4 meno dei

Activity B

1 Qualcuno; 2 Nessuno; qualcosa

Review

Activity A

1 Mi; 2 si; 3 Ci; 4 Ti

Challenge

io	mi	diverto
tu	ti	diverti
Lei	si	diverte
lui/lei	si	diverte
noi	ci	divertiamo
voi	vi	divertite
loro	si	divertono

Activity B

1 La camicia costa più della gonna. La gonna costa meno della camicia.; 2 I calzini costano meno del vestito. Il vestito costa più dei calzini.; 3 Il maglione costa meno delle scarpe. Le scarpe costano più del maglione. La gonna costa meno della cravatta. La cravatta costa più della gonna.

Activity C

Unit 8 Lesson 1

Activity A

1 to arrive; 2 to take; 3 to walk

Activity B

1 Alla stazione Termini; 2 Al Colosseo; 3 Possono prendere l'autobus, la metropolitana o andare a piedi; 4 Perché vuole sapere dove sono le vie e le chiese.

Lesson 2

Activity A

1 la biblioteca; la stazione della metropolitana; 3 la scuola; 4 la chiesa; 5 la stazione (ferroviaria); 6 la fermata dell'autobus; 7 la posta/l'ufficio postale; 8 il supermercato

Activity B

1 b; 2 b; 3 a; 4 b

Lesson 3

Activity A

1 Voglio prendere l'autobus. Come faccio ad arrivare alla fermata dell'autobus?; 2 Voglio prendere il treno. Come faccio ad arrivare alla stazione (ferroviaria)?; 3 Voglio prendere la metropolitana. Come faccio ad arrivare alla stazione della metropolitana?

Activity B

1 Dov'è la stazione (ferroviaria)?; 2 Come faccio ad arrivare alla stazione della metropolitana?; 3 La stazione (ferroviaria) è vicino alla scuola.; 4 Prendiamo una cartina!

Activity C

Per arrivare a Piazza Garibaldi deve andare alla fermata dell'autobus e prendere l'autobus numero nove.; 2 Per arrivare alla chiesa deve prendere il treno.

Your Turn

Scusi, devo andare alla fermata dell'autobus. Dov'è e come faccio ad arrivare là? Molte grazie.

Lesson 4

Activity A

1 vanno; 2 va; 3 andiamo; 4 vai

Activity B

1 al; 2 alla; 3 all'; 4 al; 5 allo

Activity C

1 Loro vanno al supermercato.; 2 Possible answers: Lui/lei va alla stazione (ferroviaria). Noi andiamo alla stazione.; 3 Loro vanno a scuola.; 4 Possible answers: Io vado in chiesa. Voi andate in chiesa.

Lesson 5

Activity A

1 b; 2 b; 3 b; 4 a

Activity B

17:30; 8:00

Lesson 6

Activity A

1 b; 2 d; 3 e; 4 c; 5 a

Activity B

1 a; 2 a; 3 b; 4 b

Lesson 7

Activity A

1 Il volo parte alle 12:30.; 2 Qual è l'uscita?; 3 Quanto costa il biglietto?; 4 Ci vediamo in albergo.

Activity B

1 a; 2 a; 3 b

Activity C

1 Il prossimo volo per Roma parte alle 16:15.; 2 I voli per Catania e Venezia.

Your Turn

Il volo 1699, diretto a Milano, parte alle 10:23 e arriva alle 13:30.

Lesson 8

Activity A

1 sa; 2 conosciamo; 3 sanno; 4 conosco; 5 sai; 6 conosce

Activity B

1 Io la mangio.; 2 Lei lo studia.; 3 Tu le conosci.; 4 Loro li prendono.

Your Turn

1 La conosco.; 2 Li conosco.; 3 Lo conosco.; 4 Lo conosco.

Review

Activity A

Cara Carla,
Sono a Venezia con mia madre. Domani andiamo a Verona. Sai dov'è Verona? Verona è molto bella. Mia madre la conosce bene. Poi andiamo a Roma sabato.
Un abbraccio,
Mario

Activity B

Vado; Il mio volo parte alle; all'aeroporto; biglietto; i bagagli e il passaporto; una stazione; vicino al; dietro una chiesa; voglio prendere la metropolitana

Activity C

Alfonso	Dov'è l'ufficio postale?
Stefania	Prendiamo una cartina!
Alfonso	Guarda la cartina. L'ufficio postale è a destra della biblioteca.
Stefania	Sì, è anche dietro il supermercato.
Alfonso	Questa è la fermata dell'autobus.
Stefania	Ecco l'autobus. Lo prendiamo?

Challenge

io so; tu sai; Lei sa; lui/lei sa; noi sappiamo; voi sapete; loro sanno

Unit 9 Lesson 1

Activity A   1 b; 2 b; 3 a; 4 a

Activity B   1 ha lavorato; 2 ha scritto; 3 cultura; 4 inizia

Lesson 2

Activity A

classe; il professore; studenti; giornalista; rivista; studentessa

Activity B

1 a la studentessa; b lo studente; c il professore
2 a l'ufficio; b il giornalista; c la giornalista

Lesson 3

Activity A

1 il professore; 2 la giornalista; 3 voglio fare la giornalista; 4 voglio fare la professoressa

Activity B

1 Che cosa vuole fare?; 2 Voglio fare il professore.; 3 Qual è la sua professione?; 4 Faccio il giornalista.

Your Turn   Answers may vary. Possible answers:

Buon giorno, mi chiamo Luca e faccio il giornalista. Qual è la sua professione? Faccio la professoressa. Io voglio fare il regista.

Lesson 4

Activity A   1 hai lavorato; 2 abbiamo venduto; ho spedito; 4 hanno lavorato

Activity B

1 Io ho lavorato in un ufficio.; 2 Tu hai venduto i vestiti; 3 Lei ha mangiato il pollo; 4 Voi avete finito i compiti; 5 Mary ha imparato l'italiano.; 6 Noi abbiamo spedito molte cartoline dall'Italia.

Lesson 5

Activity A   1 a proofreader; 2 2007; 3 Banca Nazionale; 4 employee; 5 some articles.

Your Turn   scritto

Lesson 6

Activity A   1 c; 2 a; 3 b; 4 b

Activity B

Your Turn

Answers may vary. Possible answers: Ho cinque impiegati: due assistenti e tre segretari. Lo stipendio è di 1200 euro al mese.

Lesson 7

Activity A

Answers may vary.

1 più difficile; 2 più facile; 3 più facile; 4 più difficile

Activity B

1 Perché vuole fare il giornalista?; 2 Mi piace aiutare.; 3 Per quanto tempo ha lavorato là?; 4 Ho lavorato là per due anni.

Lesson 8

Activity A

1 ho visto; 2 abbiamo letto; 3 ha bevuto; 4 hanno scritto; 5 hai fatto

Activity B

1 conclusa; 2 non conclusa; 3 conclusa; 4 non conclusa

Your Turn   Answers may vary. Possible answers: Studio l'italiano da tre mesi.

Review

Activity A

Activity B

1 Quando avete lavorato? Noi abbiamo lavorato ieri.; 2 Quando hai letto il libro? Io ho letto il libro il mese scorso. 3 Perché non ha mangiato la pasta? Lei non ha mangiato la pasta perché non le piace.

Activity C

1 aperto; 2 risposto; 3 detto; 4 preso; 5 visto

Activity D

1 Che cosa avete mangiato ieri?; 2 Studio l'italiano da due anni.; 3 L'anno scorso ho scritto un articolo per La Repubblica.; 4 Io e Laura abbiamo fatto molte cose.

Challenge   policeman; architect

Unit 10 Lesson 1

Activity A   1 b; 2 a; 3 b; 4 b

Activity B

1 Sì, l'aiuta.; 2 Non vuole spolverare.; 3 Vuole sistemare l'armadio.; 4 Dice che possono pulire e imbiancare insieme.

Lesson 2

Activity A

Answers will vary. Possible answers:

Amico   Abiti in una casa o in un **appartamento**?
Io   Abito in **una casa**.
Amico   Quante **camere/stanze** ci sono?
Io   Ci sono **quattro camere/stanze**.
Amico   Quali sono **le camere/stanze** più grandi?
Io   Le camere più grandi sono **la camerca da letto e il soggiorno**.

Activity B

1 il soggiorno; 2 la cucina; 3 la camera da letto; 4 il bagno; 5 la sala da pranzo; 6 l'armadio

Lesson 3

Activity A

1 Puoi aiutarmi?; 2 No, non posso aiutarti.; 3 Cosa vuoi che faccia?; 4 Subito.

Activity B

1 Puoi aiutarmi?; 2 Sì, posso aiutarti. Cosa vuoi che faccia?; 3 Sistema i vestiti!; 4 Subito.

Lesson 4

Activity A

1 Imbianca la stanza!; 2 Sistema l'armadio!; 3 Pulite il pavimento!

Activity B

1 Puoi; 2 puoi; 3 potete

Lesson 5

Activity A

1 a; 2 b; 3 a; 4 b

Activity B

1 È stata una bella settimana.; 2 Sono stati a un concerto di musica rock.; 3 È andata in discoteca.; 4 È andata con il suo ragazzo.

Activity C

1 È stata a un concerto di musica rock.; 2 È andata a comprare dei vestiti con sua madre.; 3 È andata in discoteca con il suo ragazzo.

Lesson 6

Activity A

1 discoteca; 2 cinema; 3 teatro; 4 concerto

Activity B

1 ieri; 2 l'altro ieri; 3 la settimana scorsa; 4 ieri sera

Activity C

```
1i 2l t e a t r o
   a  l
   l  t            3b
   t  r            a   4i l c i n e m a
   r  o            l
5i e  r i s e r a   r
   e               e
   r
6i i  l f i l m
```

Lesson 7

Activity A   1 Che cosa hai fatto la settimana scorsa?; 2 Che cosa vuoi fare?; 3 Voglio uscire.; 4 Voglio stare a casa.

Activity B

1 **Roberto**   Che cosa vuoi fare stasera?
2 **Silvia**   Voglio stare a casa stasera.
3 **Roberto**   Ma io voglio uscire di casa. Vuoi andare a ballare?
4 **Silvia**   Sono andata a ballare con i miei amici ieri.
5 **Roberto**   Andiamo al cinema?
6 **Silvia**   Sono andata al cinema ieri sera.
7 **Roberto**   Va bene, stiamo a casa stasera. Roberto decide di stare a casa stasera.

Your Turn   Answer will vary. Possible answer: **Stasera voglio stare a casa e vedere un film.**

Lesson 8

Activity A   1 è andata; 2 è stato; 3 sono nate; 4 siamo rimasti/e

Activity B   1 sono rimasto/a; 2 è nato; 3 sono andate; 4 sono venuti

Activity C   1 I stayed home yesterday.; 2 My grandfather was born on June 2nd, 1930.; 3 Giulia and Paola went to the movies last night.; 4 Marcello and Luigi came to visit me after class.

Your Turn   Answers will vary. Possible answers: **Sono nato/a negli Stati Uniti. Ieri sera sono andato/a al cinema.**

Review

Activity A   1 bagno; 2 film; 3 ballare; 4 imbiancare; 5 cucina

Activity B   1 b; 2 a; 3 b; 4 a

Activity C   1 Oggi sono rimasto/a a casa.; 2 Sei andato/a al cinema dopo cena?; 3 Silvia e Paola sono andate al supermercato.; 4 Paola è stata in Italia.

Activity D   1 Aiuta la mamma in cucina!; 2 Sistemate la vostra camera!; 3 Prenda le cose da terra!; 4 Imbianchiamo la camera!

Challenge   Answers will vary.

Unit 11 Lesson 1

Activity A

1 a; 2 b; 3 b; 4 b

Activity B

1 a; 2 b; 3 a

Activity C

Ciao Maria. Voglio giocare lunedì. Va bene?

Lesson 2

Activity A

1 il nuoto; 2 il tennis; 3 il calcio; 4 il ciclismo

Activity B

1 la palestra; 2 peso; 3 grasso; 4 magra, sana; 5 stressato/stressata; 6 malato

Activity C

1 b; 2 a; 3 a; 4 b

Lesson 3

Activity A

1 Mi sento bene.; 2 Voglio essere in forma.; 3 Come si sente?; 4 Voglio perdere peso.

Activity B

1 a; 2 a; 3 b; 4 b; 5 b

Your Turn Answers will vary. Possible answer:

Mi sento bene. Sono in forma.

Lesson 4

Activity A

1 Lui scriverà.; 2 Io ballerò.; 3 Loro studieranno.; 4 Noi partiremo.; 5 Tu conoscerai.; 6 Voi correrete.

Activity B

2 Quando studierete per l'esame?; 3 Dove correrai?; 4 Dove ballerete?; 5 Quando pulirai la tua stanza?; 6 Che cosa scriverà Luisa?

Your Turn

Pioverà.; Loro cucineranno.; 3 Lui pulirà.; 4 Lei scriverà.

Lesson 5

Activity A   1 a; 2 a; 3 b; 4 a

Activity B   1 b; 2 b; 3 a; 4 b; 5 a

Activity C

La medicina per il raffreddore combatte la febbre e la tosse e la medicina per la tosse combatte il mal di gola. La medicina per la tosse allevia la febbre e la medicina per il raffreddore allevia la febbre.

Lesson 6

Activity A

1 b; 2 b; 3 a; 4 a; 5 b

Activity B

1 Lui ha mal di pancia.; 2 Lei ha il raffreddore.; 3 Lui ha mal di testa.; 4 Lei ha mal di denti.

Your Turn

Answers will vary. Possible answers: Lui ha la febbre. Ha bisogno della medicina per il raffreddore e della medicina per la tosse.

Lesson 7

Activity A

1 Mi fa male la mano.; 2 Le fa male la schiena.; 3 Mi fanno male i piedi.; 4 Gli fa male il braccio.

Activity B

Answers may vary. Possible answers: Sono malata. Ho la febbre. Ho mal di testa e mi fa male la schiena.

Activity C

Answers may vary. Possible answers: Laura ha la febbre. Ha mal di testa e le fa male la schiena. Ha bisogno di una medicina per il raffreddore e il dottore scrive una ricetta.

Lesson 8

Activity A

Answers may vary.

Activity B

1 Gioco a pallavolo qualche volta.; 2 Vado sempre in palestra.; 3 Di solito sono stressato/stressata.; 4 Gioco a tennis una volta alla settimana. 5 Non vado mai dal dottore.; 6 Corro ogni giorno.

Activity C

1 Va sempre in Italia a luglio?; 2 Viaggia durante l'estate di solito?; 3 Pranza a casa ogni giorno Massimo?

Your Turn

Answers may vary.

Review

Activity A

Mi sento bene.; Non ho mai mal di testa.; Non andrò dal dentista.; Ho mal di pancia.; Non voglio andare dal dottore.; Faccio ginnastica perché voglio perdere peso.

Activity B

1 Mi fa male la testa.; 2 Mi fa male il braccio.; 3 Non vado mai in palestra.; 4 Teresa corre sempre nel parco.; 5 Laura cucinerà domani.; 6 Mi fanno male i piedi.

Activity C

1 ciclismo; 2 tennis; 3 mal di testa; 4 medicina; 5 febbre; 6 Dentista

Challenge

Answers may vary. Possible answers:
Domani cucinerà mio figlio.
Di solito vado al cinema.
Partirò per l'Italia.

Photo Credits

Interior

p. 8: (TR) © Jason Stitt 2008/Shutterstock, Inc., (RC) © Jason Stitt 2008/ Shutterstock,Inc., (BR) © Edyta Pawlowska 2008/Shutterstock, Inc., (TL) © Orange Line Media2008/Shutterstock, Inc., **p. 9:** (TR) © Yuri Arcurs 2008/ Shutterstock, Inc., (TRC) ©Dmitriy Shironosov 2008/Shutterstock, Inc., (BRC) © 2008 Jupiter Images, Inc., (BR)© 2008 Jupiter Images, Inc., **p. 10:** (TL) © Raia 2008/Shutterstock, Inc., (B, Bkgrd)© Lars Christensen 2008/Shutterstock, Inc., (BL, Inset) © Awe Inspiring Images2008/Shutterstock, Inc., (BLC, Inset) © Alhovik 2010/Shutterstock, Inc., (BRC,Inset) © Alhovik 2010/Shutterstock, Inc., (BR, Inset) Kripke 2010/Shutterstock, Inc., (TR)© ZTS 2008/Shutterstock, Inc., **p. 11:** (TL) © Lisa F. Young 2008/Shutterstock, Inc., (TR) © 2008 Jupiter Images, Inc., (CL) © BobbyDeal 2008/Shutterstock, Inc., (CLC) © 2008Jupiter Images, Inc., (CRC) © Yuri Arcurs 2008/Shutterstock, Inc., (BLL) © 2008Jupiter Images, Inc., (BL) © Yuri Arcurs 2008/Shutterstock, Inc., (BLC) ©Konstantynov 2008/ Shutterstock, Inc., (BR) © Andresr 2008/Shutterstock, Inc., **p.13:** (TL) © Sandra G 2008/Shutterstock, Inc., (TR) © Nayashkova Olga 2010/Shutterstock, Inc., (TRC) © Lukas Wroblewski 2008/Shutterstock, Inc., (CRT) © Tatiana Popova 2010/Shutterstock, Inc., (CRB) © Edyta Pawlowska 2008/Shutterstock, Inc., (BLT) © photobank.ch 2008/Shutterstock, Inc., (BLC) © Supri Suharjoto 2008/ Shutterstock, Inc., (BL) © 2008 Jupiter Images, Inc., (BLB) © Niels Quist 2008/ Shutterstock, Inc., (BRC) © Daniel Wiedemann 2008/Shutterstock, Inc., **p. 14:** (C) ©Raphael Ramirez Lee 2008/Shutterstock, Inc., (B) © Javier Larrea/Pixtal/ AgeFotostock, **p. 15:** (T) © Yuri Arcurs 2008/Shutterstock, Inc., (B) © DmitriyShironosov 2008/Shutterstock, Inc., **p. 16:** © Karl Weatherly 2010/ Agefotostock, **p. 17:** (TL, Inset) © Pavel Sazonov 2008/Shutterstock, Inc., (TLC, Inset) © PIXTAL. All rights reserved, (TRC, Inset) © Matt Ragen 2010/Shutterstock, Inc., (TR, Inset) © Khoroshunova Olga 2008/Shutterstock, Inc., (BLL, Inset) © Jurijs Korjakins 2010/Shutterstock, Inc., (BL, Inset) © Danilo Ascione 2010/ Shutterstock, Inc., (BRC, Inset) © Martina Ebel 2010/Shutterstock, Inc., (BR, Inset) © Elena Elisseeva 2008/Shutterstock,Inc., (BR) © Kiselev Andrey Valerevich 2008/Shutterstock, Inc., **p. 18:** (TLL) © photobank.ch 2008/Shutterstock, Inc., (TLC)© Yuri Arcurs 2008/Shutterstock, Inc., (TLR) © vgstudio 2008/Shutterstock, Inc., (TR, Bkgrd) © iofoto 2008/Shutterstock, Inc., (TR, Inset) © Stacy Barnett 2008/Shutterstock, Inc., (CLL) © BESTWEB 2008/Shutterstock, Inc., (CLC) © Lexx 2008/Shutterstock, Inc., (CLR) © Alexey Nikolaew 2008/Shutterstock, Inc., (B) © VibrantImage Studio 2008/Shutterstock, Inc., (BLL) © Vladimir Melnik 2008/Shutterstock,Inc., (BLC) © Denise Kappa 2008/Shutterstock, Inc., (BLR) © Jurijs Korjakins 2010/Shutterstock, Inc., (BCL) © fckncg 2008/Shutterstock, Inc., (BCR) © Hannu Lilvaar2008/Shutterstock, Inc., (R, Bkgrd) © Arthur Eugene Preston 2008/Shutterstock, Inc., (LL, Inset) © Kristian Sekulic 2008/Shutterstock, Inc., (LC, Inset) © Sandy MayaMatzen 2008/Shutterstock, Inc., (C, Inset) © Galina Barskaya 2008/Shutterstock,Inc., (RC, Inset) © Rob Wilson 2008/ Shutterstock, Inc., (RR, Inset) © Luminis 2008/Shutterstock, Inc., **p. 19:** (T) © Nagy-Bagoly Arpad 2008/Shutterstock, Inc., (L) ©Yuri Arcurs 2008/Shutterstock, Inc., (CL) © Dmitriy Shironosov 2008/Shutterstock,Inc., (CRL) © Erik Lam 2008/ Shutterstock, Inc., (CRC) © Suponev VladimirMihajlovich 2008/Shutterstock, Inc., (CRR) © mlorenz 2008/Shutterstock, Inc., (B)© Vaclav Volrab 2008/Shutterstock, Inc., **p. 20:** (TL) © Andresr 2008/Shutterstock, Inc., (TR) © Ustyujanin 2008/ Shutterstock, Inc., (CL) © Andrey Armyagov 2008/Shutterstock, Inc., (CRL) © MargoHarrison 2008/Shutterstock, Inc., (CR) © Yuri Arcurs 2008/Shutterstock, Inc., (CRR)© Hannu Lilvaar 2008/Shutterstock, Inc., (CRB) © melkerw 2008/ Shutterstock, Inc., (BL) © pandapaw 2008/Shutterstock, Inc., (BLC) © Rafa Irusta 2008/Shutterstock,Inc., (BR) © Kiselev Andrey Valerevich 2008/Shutterstock, Inc., **p. 21:** © SamDCruz 2008/Shutterstock, Inc., **p. 22:** (TL) © Scott Waldron 2008/Shutterstock, Inc., (BR) © Jason Stitt 2008/Shutterstock, Inc., **p. 23:** (TL) © 2008 Jupiter Images, Inc., (TR) © J2008 upiter Images, Inc., (TRC) © J2008 upiter Images, Inc., (C) © DavidGilder 2008/Shutterstock, Inc., (BL) © Andy Lim 2008/Shutterstock, Inc., (BRC) ©J2008 upiter Images, Inc., (BR) © J2008 upiter Images, Inc., **p. 24:** (TL) © 2008Jupiter Images, Inc., (TR) © Monkey Business Images 2008/Shutterstock, Inc., (RC) ©Andrejs Pidjass 2008/ Shutterstock, Inc., (BR) © Donna Heatfield 2008/Shutterstock,Inc., **p. 25:** (TL) © Nick Stubbs 2008/Shutterstock, Inc., (TLC) © Daniela Mangiuca2008/ Shutterstock, Inc., (TR) © Vladimir Mucibabic 2008/Shutterstock, Inc., (LCL) © Lexx 2010/Shutterstock, Inc., (LCR) © Lexx 2010/Shutterstock, Inc., (LC) © Philip Date 2008/Shutterstock, Inc., (BL) © Raia 2008/Shutterstock, Inc., **p. 26:** (T, Bkgrd) © yurok 2008/Shutterstock, Inc., (T, Inset) ©2008 Jupiter Images, Inc., (L, Inset) © Stephen Mcsweeny 2008/Shutterstock, Inc., (R) © Steve Luker 2008/ Shutterstock, Inc., (R, Inset) © Tatiana Strelkova 2008/Shutterstock, Inc., (C, Inset) © Michelle Marsan 2008/Shutterstock, Inc., (CR) ©MaxFX 2008/ Shutterstock, Inc., (BC) © MaxFX 2008/Shutterstock, Inc., (BRC) ©Steve Luker 2008/Shutterstock, Inc., (BR) © Bart Everett 2008/Shutterstock, Inc., **p.27:** (TL) © Andresr 2008/Shutterstock, Inc., (TR) © laurent hamels 2008/Shutterstock, Inc., (BR) © Fatini Zulnaidi 2008/Shutterstock, Inc., **p. 28:** (TL) ©Konstantin Remizov 2008/Shutterstock, Inc., **p. 29:** (TR) © Srdjan Nikolich 2010/ Shutterstock, Inc., (TRC) © Jenn Mackenzie 2010/Shutterstock, Inc., (RC) © nikkytok 2010/Shutterstock, Inc., (BRC) © Stephen Coburn 2010/Shutterstock, Inc., **p. 30:** (T) © Rafa Irusta 2008/Shutterstock, Inc., (TL) © GinaSanders 2008/Shutterstock, Inc., (TLC) © 2008 Jupiter Images, Inc., (TRC) © iofoto2008/ Shutterstock, Inc., (TR) © Morgan Lane Photography 2008/Shutterstock, Inc., (CL) © tinatka 2008/Shutterstock, Inc., (CR) © Elena Ray 2008/Shutterstock, Inc., (BL) © George Dolgikh 2008/Shutterstock, Inc., (BC) © David Hyde 2008/ Shutterstock, Inc., (BRC) © J. Helgason 2008/Shutterstock, Inc., (BR) © JulianRovagnati 2008/Shutterstock, Inc., **p. 32:** (TR) © Gelpi 2008/ Shutterstock, Inc., (RC)© 2008 Jupiter Images, Inc., (B) © Phil Date 2008/ Shutterstock, Inc., **p. 33:** (T) © © Imageshop.com, (TRC) © Simone van den Berg 2008/Shutterstock, Inc., (TR) © 2008 Jupiter Images, Inc., (BRC) © Edyta Pawlowska 2010/Shutterstock, Inc., (BR) © Kzenon 2010/Shutterstock, Inc., (BLC) © Tomasz Trojanowski 2008/Shutterstock, Inc., **p. 34:** (BL) © Mike Flippo 2008/Shutterstock, Inc., (BR) © Pakhnyushcha2008/Shutterstock, Inc., **p. 35:** (T) © Christian Wheatley 2008/Shutterstock, Inc., (TL) © Simon Krzic 2008/ Shutterstock, Inc., (TLC) © Edyta Pawlowska 2008/Shutterstock, Inc., (TC) © MWProductions 2008/Shutterstock, Inc., (TRC) © DusaleevViatcheslav 2008/ Shutterstock, Inc., (TR) © Olga Lyubkina 2008/Shutterstock, Inc., **p. 36:** (CL) © Andresr 2008/Shutterstock, Inc., (CR) © T-Design 2008/Shutterstock,Inc., (B) © Ivan Jelisavic 2008/Shutterstock, Inc., (BL) © Jason Stitt 2008/Shutterstock, Inc., (BR) © Dimitrije Paunovic 2008/Shutterstock, Inc., (Bkgrd) © khz2008/ Shutterstock, Inc., **p. 37:** (TL) © Vibrant Image Studio 2008/Shutterstock, Inc., (TR) © Ersler Dmitry 2008/Shutterstock, Inc., (TRC) © Jeanne Hatch 2008/ Shutterstock, Inc., (L) © iofoto 2008/Shutterstock, Inc., (CL) © iofoto 2008/ Shutterstock, Inc., (BL) © iofoto 2008/Shutterstock, Inc., (BRC) © Jaren Jai Wicklund2008/Shutterstock, Inc., (BR) © Adam Borkowski 2008/Shutterstock, Inc., **p. 38:** (TL)© Lisa F. Young 2008/Shutterstock, Inc., (TRC) © Martin Valigursky 2008/Shutterstock, Inc., (TR) © Monkey Business Images 2008/ Shutterstock, Inc., (RCT) ©Vibrant Image Studio 2008/Shutterstock, Inc., (RCB) © Monkey Business Images2008/Shutterstock, Inc., (R) © Sonya Etchison 2008/ Shutterstock, Inc., (BRC) ©Denise Kappa 2008/Shutterstock, Inc., (BR) © Monkey Business Images 2008/Shutterstock, Inc., **p. 39:** (TL) © Evgeny V. Kan 2008/ Shutterstock, Inc., (TR) © CarmeBalcells 2008/Shutterstock, Inc., (L) © Sandra G 2008/Shutterstock, Inc., (LC) ©Kurhan 2008/Shutterstock, Inc., (RC) © Simon Krzic 2008/Shutterstock, Inc., (C) ©Konstantin Sutyagin 2008/Shutterstock, Inc., (R) © Carme Balcells 2008/Shutterstock, Inc., (BL) © Lexx 2008/Shutterstock, Inc., (BLC) © Allgord 2008/Shutterstock, Inc., (BRC) © Sandra G 2008/ Shutterstock, Inc., (BR) © AndriyGoncharenko 2008/Shutterstock, Inc., (BBL) © Dagmara Ponikiewska 2008/Shutterstock, Inc., (BBR) © KSR 2008/Shutterstock, Inc., **p. 40:** (TL) © Lisa F. Young2008/Shutterstock, Inc., (B) © Elena Ray 2008/ Shutterstock, Inc., (BL) © Najin2008/Shutterstock, Inc., (BR) © Elena Ray 2008/ Shutterstock, Inc., **p. 41:** (TL) ©Losevsky Pavel 2008/Shutterstock, Inc., (TR) © Ustyujanin 2008/Shutterstock, Inc., (B) © Elena Ray 2008/Shutterstock, Inc., (BL) © Elena Ray 2008/Shutterstock, Inc., (BLC) © Vitezslav Halamka 2008/ Shutterstock, Inc., (BRC) © Vitezslav Halamka2008/Shutterstock, Inc., (BR) © Robin Mackenzie 2008/Shutterstock, Inc., **p. 42:** (TL)© Serghei Starus 2008/ Shutterstock, Inc., (TLC) © Jurijs Korjakins 2010/Shutterstock, Inc., (BL) © Rui Vale de Sousa 2008/Shutterstock, Inc., (BLC) © Tonis Valing 2010/Shutterstock, Inc., (BR) © 2008 Jupiter Images, Inc., **p. 43:** (TL) ©Monkey Business Images 2008/ Shutterstock, Inc., (TR) © Sandra G 2008/Shutterstock, Inc., (BL) © Monkey Business Images 2008/Shutterstock, Inc., (BR) ©Konstantin Sutyagin 2008/ Shutterstock, Inc., **p. 44:** (TL) © Sergey Rusakov 2008/Shutterstock, Inc., (TLC) © Joe Gough 2008/Shutterstock, Inc., (TR) © RexRover 2008/Shutterstock, Inc., (TRC) © Valentyn Volkov 2008/Shutterstock, Inc., (CR) © Rudchenko Liliia 2008/ Shutterstock, Inc., (R) © imageZebra 2008/Shutterstock, Inc., (BL) © Ljupco Smokovski 2008/Shutterstock, Inc., (BLC) © Peter Polak 2008/Shutterstock, Inc., (BRC) © Edyta Pawlowska 2008/Shutterstock, Inc., (BR) © Edyta Pawlowska 2008/Shutterstock, Inc., **p. 45:** (TL) © Edyta Pawlowska 2008/Shutterstock, Inc., (TRC) © Dusan Zidar 2008/Shutterstock, Inc., (TR) © SupriSuharjoto 2008/ Shutterstock, Inc., (R) © Edw 2008/Shutterstock, Inc., (RC) ©Monkey Business Images 2008/Shutterstock, Inc., (BLC) © Nayashkova Olga 2010/Shutterstock, Inc., (BR) © 2008 Jupiter Images, Inc., **p. 46:** (TL) © Ana Blazic 2008/ Shutterstock, Inc., (TR) © Alexander Shalamov 2008/Shutterstock, Inc., (R) © Phil Date 2008/Shutterstock, Inc., (BR) © Dragan Trifunovic2008/Shutterstock, Inc., **p. 47:** (TL) © Steve Luker 2008/Shutterstock, Inc., **p. 48:** (TL) © 2008 Jupiter Images, Inc., (TLC)© Viktor1 2008/Shutterstock, Inc., (TRC) © a9photo 2010/ Shutterstock,Inc., (LC) © Anna Nizami 2008/Shutterstock, Inc., (B) © AndrejsPidjass 2008/Shutterstock, Inc., (BL) © Sarune Zurbaite 2008/ Shutterstock, Inc., (BLC) © Bochkarev Photography 2008/Shutterstock, Inc., (BRC) © Liv Friis-Larsen2008/Shutterstock, Inc., (BR) © Kheng Guan Toh 2008/ Shutterstock, Inc., **p. 49:** (TL)© Rene Jansa 2008/Shutterstock, Inc., (TRC) © Stephanie Frey 2010/Shutterstock, Inc., (TR) © Valentin Mosichev 2008/ Shutterstock, Inc., (CR) © Olga Lyubkina 2008/Shutterstock, Inc., (R) © Joe Gough 2008/Shutterstock, Inc., (BL) © 2008 JupiterImages, Inc., (BRC) © Paul Maguire 2008/Shutterstock, Inc., (BR) © Viktor1 2008/Shutterstock, Inc., **p. 50:** (TL) © 2008 Jupiter Images, Inc., (BR) © Keith Wheatley 2008/Shutterstock, Inc., **p. 51:** (TL)© Lisa F. Young 2008/Shutterstock, Inc., (BL) © David P. Smith 2008/Shutterstock,Inc., (BLC) © Dusan Zidar 2008/Shutterstock, Inc., (BRC) © David P. Smith 2008/Shutterstock, Inc., (BR) © Monkey Business Images 2008/ Shutterstock, Inc., **p. 52:** (TL)© Stepanov 2008/Shutterstock, Inc., (TLC) © Ilker Canikligil 2008/Shutterstock, Inc., (CL) © Joe Gough 2008/Shutterstock, Inc., (CLC) © Bjorn Heller 2008/Shutterstock,Inc., (R) © Darren Baker 2008/